MW00709759

Dr. Vali's

SURVIVAL GUIDE:

Tips For The Journey

Dr. Vali's SURVIVAL GUIDE:

Tips For The Journey

Vali Hawkins Mitchell, Ph.D.

An Emerald of Siam Book

FIRST EDITION Published in 1999.

Library of Congress Cataloging-in Publication-Data

Mitchell, Vali Hawkins.

Dr. Vali's Survivor Guide: Tips for the Journey / Vali Hawkins Mitchell.—1st ed.

p.   cm.

ISBN 0-9628783-2-4

Library of Congress Catalog Number 98-94862

1. Inspiration. 2. Soul Choices. 3. Surviving Trauma.

I. Title.

Book Design and production by David Mitchell, Inner Directions

"We who lived in concentration camps can remember the men who walked through the huts comforting others, giving away their last piece of bread. They may have been few in number, but they offer sufficient proof that everything can be taken from a man but one thing: the last of the human freedoms – to choose one's attitude in any given set of circumstances, to choose one's own way."

– Viktor E. Frankl

Contents

Acknowledgments

Version 1: The Novel

This book would not exist if it wasn't for my precious husband David and his faith. (You are my angel and my Star of Bethlehem.) I also thank Vicki Grayland, editor and world class photojournalist, for having faith in me as a writer and a friend. Thanks to my publisher, Ravadi, for her generous gifts of soul and food.

So many angels have offered light through dark times but I especially thank my friends in Florence and Chuck Carter for the cheese grater on my worst day ever, Ivy Comara, Cindy and Jay Cable, Ellen and Eliot Diamond, Carol Foster for a job near books and therapy dogs, Laura Merz, and Eva, Marla, Margaret for elevating me above counter scum. I appreciate my writing students, everyone who was there when I shaved my head and my Methodist Family.

Thanks also to precious sisters Auntie Sonnie and Wendie who got custody of me, Gerald Rafferty for the Arizona laughter, Jim's surprise gifts, Ed and Hannah,

Sharon's Rosary and Jen's Umbrella. To my Grandma Grace and Dad. Humble thanks to all my clients who have survived life on life's terms, all survivors of all Holocausts and strangers who did the little things that got me here, like post office pals and police officers, all firefighters, the nurse who put her hand on my head, and the cook who gave me extra potatoes and gravy on the day my baby had surgery and just knew I needed more comfort food and didn't even ask but just plopped more on my plate with that special sad smile that said, "I know you are hurting," and to all sweepers who remind me of my place in life no matter where or what time it is on the planet. Thanks to the children of my best friend and the creators of Christmas movies that show cranky adults rediscovering their hearts, to Catherine Ponder, Walt Disney, my professors who demanded I not lose my soul for a degree, to Fresh Aire II and my cats who stayed alive for 19 years until I was safe. Thank you to the Mommies of sick and dying babies who gave me strength in their own hours of darkness, and to the doctor who cried with me.

More recent angels include Judge Dennis Yule who officially ruled my words were poetic, entertaining and charming and not the work of Satan, to Dr. Sheila Dunlop for our weekly Pair-a-Docs conference. Thanks for making me feel at home to Shauna and Rudy, Doug and Aggie, Tim and Kim, and the world's best in-laws Dean and Helen. Smoodgie thanks to the Little Missy, Ashley, for her intuition, wit and karate chops.

Okay, now I know why those academy award shows are so long, appropriate gratitude really does matter and I know I have forgotten someone and none of us get here alone. Finally, here's a huge special big-heart-dancing-in-the-wind-while-we-are-wearing-our matching-magic-socks thanks to my mostest, bestest pal in the entire world and probably universe, Donna Wendling, who helps me survive on a daily basis. And to Kyrin Aerie who changed my life completely one morning.

And, oh, did I mention my **Awesome God?**

Version 2: The Matchbook Cover

THANKS TO EVERYBODY....COULDN'T HAVE DONE IT WITHOUT YA.......LOVE, VALI

Dedication

For my daughters Kyrin Aerie and Kirsha Melanie
who taught me the meaning of Soul Survival

Introduction

When I began writing the **Oregon Coast Survival Guide** for INKFISH Magazine I did not expect to continue writing the column for 3 years. I also did not expect it to be renamed **Soul Survivor** by the editor in response to my experiences after the death of my 21 year old daughter. I also didn't expect to get fan mail. But life is full of surprises, isn't it? And it's not the surprises which give us character, it's what we do with those unexpected events that makes a difference.

Have you ever seen a family home after an earthquake or tornado? I remember seeing a place where someone had put a tablecloth across their own personal pile of rubble and offered dinner to the neighborhood. Now that is survival at its highest and most graceful level. That kind of blessing to themselves and to their neighbors is the stuff of miracles. If we can turn our tragedies into miracles then we have risen above the mundane and moved into the soulful. One of my heroes, Viktor Frankl, wrote a book entitled, *Man's Search for Meaning*. He was a Holocaust survivor who found that it was in the act of making meaning out of the madness which paved the way to survival. There are so many stories about heroism in everyday life that sometimes we forget

1

that it is that very "everyday life" we are trying to survive. Everyone I have ever met has had their own mountain to climb and their own story of survival and heroism. Often I find people defining their victories in terms of minimalism. "Oh, gee," they say, "There are others who have it so much rougher than me." Even if that is true that kind of thinking degrades the journey. One man's hill is another man's mountain and vice versa. Survival isn't a contest against each other in terms of oneupmanship. Survival is a group challenge and everyone is playing and we are all on the same team called Humanity.

As I continue my work as a counselor and workshop presenter, I expect to encounter many other survivors with familiar and new stories about their efforts to make meaning out of the madness of their survival journey. As I continue my life I expect to encounter many other challenges on my own journey. Big deal. My journey is mine and I will make of it what I make of it. And you will also. In the following pages you will see some of the reflections of my journey notes. What you will have to read between the lines is the specifics of what I was doing at the time.....breaking up with a lover? Getting a Divorce? Graduating my daughter from high school? Falling in Love? Getting married? Having surgery for possible cancer? Cremating my first born child? Finishing up my PhD? Losing my job? Failing? Succeeding? Running? Moving away? Joy? Terror? Romance?

Life. Survival. All that and more is inside this little collection of words. It's between the lines and beyond the words. Perhaps you can find a few moments of honesty and peace and whimsy inside.

Dr. Vali's reading tip de jour

Put on some cozy socks, grab a bowl of tapioca or other such gooey snack, turn on some favorite music, unplug the phone or head for the garden or settle under a tree or float on an air mattress while you contemplate some survival tips. Feel free to add your own tips to the list. That way you can offer your journey wisdom to the next person who needs some handy dandy tips for surviving life on life's terms. And since life is all we really have while we are here, I suggest you pay attention to it as it zips past you like the great wind. Stand tall with your arms outstretched and feel the wind blow through the holes in your soul and sing the songs of the universe with a loud and joyous and angry and vital and soulful and magical and fearful and whimsical and silly and delightful and holy voice.

Soul Survivors

When I was young I would run to the shore
in search of the perfect shell.

Now I walk my beaches in gratitude
for each precious fragment.

I have learned to value survivors.

Chapter 1

Introduction to Survival

Welcome to the Survival Guide. My name is Dr. Vali and I will be your tour guide for a while. (Please put your trays up in the locked position and keep your hands inside the tram at all times.)

Survival is often a messy business. People who have survived life traumas and tribulations will attest to the fact that it is very difficult to survive. And those who can look graceful at the same time are rare. However, once a person has determined that they have indeed survived, there is a tendency to be very grateful. And that is the essence of grace.

Some handy-dandy Definitions:

Survival: (Dr. Vali)
There are three kinds of survival: (1) The little day-to-day-how-to-have-a-wonderful-life-with-

all-its-ups-and-downs-ins-and-outs-highs-and-lows-type of hanging in there; (2) The grab-your-babies-and-photo-albums-and-alfalfa-sprout-seeds-and-head-for-high-ground-or-the-hills-to-survive-the-coming-catastrophes-and-do-you-have-the-number-for-the-Red-Cross survival; and (3) The something-unexpected-has-happened-and-I-must-make-a-soul-choice survival

Guide: (Dr. Vali)

To point out scenery and other points of interest along the way

Magic Princess Ring: (Dr. Vali)

A ring that when worn and used correctly allows the wearer to be transported wherever she wants so she feels like a magical princess

Magic Prince Ring: (Dr. Vali)

Same as above only usually a bigger size, and generally used to transport a magical prince

Imagination: (Dr. Vali)

Essential to survival because sometimes reality is too harsh to look at square in the face

Grace: (Dr. Vali)

My Grandma's name and a state of undeserved blessing accompanied by gratitude and serenity

Let me introduce myself and offer my survival resume in brief so you know why I got this job as your guide. I am a world class survivor. Within the frame of my life I have survived a nearly disastrous childhood due to the fact that I was raised by wolves. My young adulthood was a series of catastrophes of violence and terror. As I moved into my life as a parent I gave birth to two children challenged with life threatening illness and spent years sleeping on lumpy cots beside baby beds in pediatric units in hospitals. I have lost everything I owned several times, been homeless, married and divorced, hung out with death, and moved from the welfare rolls with no education to completing a Ph.D. And these are just some of the high points. Everyone has their own mountains to climb and the details of my survival are personal and important mostly to myself and my God. But what qualifies me for this job as Tour Guide is that I know there is a secret to the journey. Survival can be a horror or an adventure.

In a crisis there are two doorways marked Survival. One is marked Light and the other is marked Victim. The main secret to Surviving the Journey is to deeply and fully honor the darkness of an experience, then choose the Light to survive it with grace. This does not mean turn your trauma into whimsy. In fact, it means take it so seriously that you can qualify as an experienced Tour Guide for those who are just starting out. Use your soul's best wisdom on your trip and develop your own Magic Ring of Imagination. Turn Darkness into Light.

Let's go. The journey of survival takes a while, so let's not waste anymore time. Peer deeply into my Magic Princess Ring so I can show you some scenery from my Journey. Feel free to point out things you see also, because we are all on this trip together.

Survival tips de jour

1. Be prepared for life changes, Keep an umbrella in the car. But also keep sun glasses.
2. Make up names for things that confuse you.
3. Have dinner leftovers by candlelight. Or eat cold cereal at the beach.
4. Buy a special blanket for snuggling when you are left alone. Sing.
5. Get a wind-friendly hairdo that can survive hurricanes. Laugh as much as you can.
6. Practice being a cheap date, or at least easily entertained so that you are good company.
7. Sit under a tree with your Cell Phone and call your mostest bestest pal and say Thank You a lot.
8. Get up one more time than you fall down.
9. Write. Share good news.
10. Celebrate the next 5 minutes of your life as a miracle.

Chapter 2

The Art of Listening

The Magic Princess Ring transported me to Nevada last week to hear my daughter perform in the symphony. While away I indulged in many other out-of-town-sounds. I listened to airport cacophony, slot machine screamers, honking horn limos, screeching pavement taxis, shopping mall grindings, tourist tantrums, and crisp edges of palm leaves crackling in hot wind. When I heard a cute little gentleman laughing I realized that creative listening is a nifty survival skill that serves me well. It is always good to get home to comfortable and familiar sounds.

Some handy-dandy Definitions:

Listen: (Dr. Vali)
   To pay attention with the ears. (Which is different than paying attention TO ears as we do when viewing Prince Charles or Ross Perot.)

Cacophony: (Dr. Vali)
Jarring, discordant and harsh sound (Like 37 toddlers at a chalk board accompanied by a marching band in corduroy pants and tap shoes playing off-key Sousa Marches inside a shopping mall on the first exchange day after Christmas.) (Ouch!)
Myopic: (Dr. Vali)
Shortsighted (visually shortsheeted)

To survive joyfully in Our Festive Little Universe, one must creatively make use of as many senses as one has available. This can include the sense of hearing in an effort to avoid being audibly-myopic. (We can close our eyes but we have to plug our ears.) I was raised by wolves, so I had to pay attention to the slightest inflection of tone to determine the temperament of the day. The fact that the wolves were musicians added a pesky dimension to the daily ear brew. Thus, when my babies were little, I would put little record players beside their cribs with cheap yet tender recordings of the classics. Now I crack the windows open to hear the live performances of rain concerts off the eaves. Kitchen percussion is an art form at our house and we listen for the sounds of bird chirping revelry, clock ticking lullabies, chain saw hymns, lawn mowing gavottes and new-construction opera.

We listen to survive. We pay attention if someone runs into a local beachside coffee shop and yells "the surf is up," or "the tide has turned," or "the fish are biting," or "the coffee's ready," or "someone is hiring down the road." We listen to survive. I recall the first time I lived directly on the Pacific Coast (440 feet from the sea line) and someone

10

said, "A big blow is coming, better batten down the hatches."
Gosh, I thought that was so darn cute and locally quaint...
Until the wind blew 102 miles per hour! The next time I
listened and battened those pesky little hatches!!! And do
the words earthquake, flood, tornado, hurricane, fire or
tsunami just perk up local antennae? People who listen to
police scanners always seemed rudely voyeuristic to me
until there was that enormous fire in the neighborhood, and
everyone listening came to see what they could do to help.

I went to college far inland and missed sea sounds. I
would often walk to class across a large field of land-gulls
(the kind who surf garbage dumps and fly over parking
lots) taking a bird-break of some sort. I would close my
eyes and listen. My other senses were transported to the
coast and I could almost feel the cold air, taste the salt and
smell the creosote-treated pilings of a favorite dock.

Listen for the sound of opportunity knocking quietly,
doors opening, doors closing, your own heartbeat, the music
of the spheres, local language and global vocabulary,
footsteps and raindrops, telephones and purring cats, children
playing and who has the remote. Listen to what is loud and
to the silence of what is not said. Can't get out of town?
Homesick? Lonely? Bored? Close your eyes for a few
moments and listen to the past and for the future.

Survival tips de jour:

1. Listen to Books on Tape, they are free from your Public Library.
2. Listen to the Wind...always. (There are countless wind sounds. Catalog them as a hobby.)
3. Listen for New ways to kill mildew or save trees or grow rhododendrons or save coyotes or find jobs or anything to help yourself or someone else. (We're all in this thing together.)
4. Attend a free concert at your local High School, Community College, or University. Sometimes it is music of young struggle, and other times, I guarantee, you will hear world class music.
5. Listen to traffic sounds.
6. Listen to the Chucka-chucka-chucka of a rescue helicopter.
7. Listen to Ocean Percussions or Mountain Opera.
8. Listen to find out where a new store is doing its Grand Opening and go for the freebies.
9. Listen to the wisdoms of that retired person sitting beside you on a plane.
10. Listen to the Wisdom of someone much younger than yourself.
11. Listen to the radio for a change of pace.
12. Listen for Laughter... Seek its source like the Holy Grail. Embrace it.

Chapter 3

Flowerspowers

I had planned to write about the adventures of moving... But I couldn't find my sense of humor having packed it in a cardboard box that I probably won't find until Saint Swithin's Day. I then started writing about my new theory of Global Harmony through Tapioca Management when a friend, who, oddly enough, does not like tapioca, thought it needed a bit more research. While meditating upon this as I was heading to the market for more pudding, I walked past the Lavender garden in front of a favorite local restaurant. I checked for bumblebees and ran my hand across the blossoms. A friend had sweetly gifted me with fresh Lavender for my new apartment and the lingering fragrance reminded me that flowers are one of my personal survival requirements.

Some handy-dandy-definitions:

Flower: (Webster)
A shoot of sporophyte of a higher plant that is modified for reproduction and consists of shortened axis bearing modified leaves.

Flower: (Disney)
    The name of a skunk
Flower: (Dr. Vali)
    Colorful and fragrant and delicate miracles that I
    get to see out my window or place on my table
Wimps: (Dr. Vali)
    People who think flowers are for sissies and have
    no respect for what it takes to become a flower
    from a little, itty-bitty, eensy-teensy seed

The Magic Princess Ring sent me to Astoria, Oregon. Up the coastline I cleverly traveled on a FRIDAY AFTERNOON IN THE HEIGHT OF TOURIST SEASON!!!!! The word grueling comes to mind. I was on a mission of soul work so I didn't take time to hang anywhere. I just kept movin' north. I would have used the Magic Princess Ring, but forgot it in the mad rush to escape my Hellish Life in Paradise. After at least 11,352,789 hours of driving I zipped past a colorful blur. I thought I was losing what was left of my mind. But after three such blurs I realized they were flower stands. Charming, but who can afford to stop and buy flowers? Wait! Did that sign say $2 a bunch? I made a harrowing U-turn. The unpersoned stand offered a simple box for money, bunches of gorgeous bouquets, and a sign that read, *"Please be honest."* (Interesting concept, eh?) My friends confirmed that this had been going on for years, the price recently up from $1 to pay for the "flower-man's" health care. (I hope someone sent him flowers.)

I often walk my neighborhood picking flowers in vacant lots and alleys. When I was a little girl I would pick rose petals and smoosh them into "perfume" for the entire "lucky"

14

family. Flower watchers watch the varieties changing from month to month, colors changing with seasons and fragrances going from light to hearty as winter approaches. From the first spring crocus to the last mum before the frosts, human beings are gifted by bursts of color which began only a few weeks earlier as ittsseee-bittseee-teensy-weensy-tinsy little (small) seeds. Not unlike Human Beings, flowers begin small and vulnerable and become different colored and shaped expressions of life. This is no small task given the variables of survival on Planet Earth. Flowers often accompany life transitions, rituals and special events. Weddings have bouquets to toss and proms have corsages to pin on strapless gowns. Ever leave a Mayday basket of flowers on a porch, ring the bell and run? Restaurants with class have fresh flowers and people who think they are way too hip or way too sophisticated to have flowers on their tables will probably get flowers at their funerals. *Kinda makes sense to enjoy them now.* The poets say "take time to smell the roses" but do a quick bee-check first since a bee up the nose is worse than a bee up your bonnet. Once an anonymous rose left under my windshield wiper warmed my normally cold heart. I sent a special someone petals in an envelope and got some back in person. Hey, when was the last time you put a rose behind your ear and danced to a Mariachi Band? Take a Sunday drive and look for wild flowers growing in rocky crevasses and on windblown hills. A mystic said, "The same stream of life that runs through the world runs through my veins night and day and dances in rhythmic measure. It is the same life that shoots in joy through the dust of the earth into numberless blades of grass and breaks into tumultuous waves of flowers." Flower power wasn't just a Hippie thing. The spirit of a Rhododendron, Rose, Lilac or Daffodil

15

Community festival is a joyous celebration with family and friends and parades and princesses. And what's more precious than a droopy dandelion bouquet picked by a toddler? And remember, a "rose by any other name" is still a rose, but a Chrysanthemum by any other name is easier to spell.

Survival tips de jour:

1. Send flowers to a loved one.
2. Pick flowers for yourself on your birthday.
3. Doodle flowers on the edges of your notebook during important meetings.
4. Plant flowers anonymously at night. (Commit Random Acts of Planting.)
5. Please protect the Indigenous Wild Flowers.
6. Remember: Real men aren't afraid of flowers, Real women aren't afraid to send them to Real men.
7. If you want to break a bad habit, put a quarter in a jar each time you blow it, then when (if) the jar gets full, take the money and send flowers anonymously to your least favorite person.
8. Support artists who paint, photograph or sculpt flowers. Go to galleries, look at their gardens.
9. Ask a flower if you can pick it. They usually say "YES." Occasionally a flower is on a mission and must be left alone to grow, to be picked by someone else, or to offer its silent beauty to the planet, decay, and release its life back to the Universe. People are that way sometimes.
10. If you win the lottery, send me flowers. From Paris.

Chapter 4

Community Donuts

In the tradition of a War Correspondent, I write you from the trenches. Bullets are flying, death is all around me, hearts are on sleeves and miracles are spontaneous. And just when I thought I was alone in my foxhole, while the fortunate rest of the world was dancing mindlessly and eating cake at the USO, a buddy runs through the fray and tosses me a donut. Holy Donut Wholes! A reminder that My Community is an essential survival element where I live. And I suspect everywhere else on the planet.

Some Handy Dandy Definitions:

Donuts: (Dr. Vali)
Cake goodies with a hole in the middle

Foxholes: (Dr. Vali)
Safety zones with a hole in the middle

17

Miracles: (Dr. Vali)
Special moments with a Whole in the middle

Community: (Dr. Vali)
Present People with a Holy in the middle

My 21 year old daughter Kirsha Melanie died unexpectedly on September 12. Police Officer John gently came to the door. (Wow, is that rough duty...) I was hoping I was overparked... Unlikely at midnight. Then, after first horrors, my best friend came. Then my other daughter Kyrin came and then the rest of my community came. With food, and hugs, and flowers, and tears and comedy, and food, and mineral water, and coffee, and music boxes, and food, and cards, and angel gifts and good hearts and food and bravery. They just sat with me. I don't know how they knew what to do but they did it. I now know the difference between soldiers and warriors. Warriors don't twitch and run... they simply stand their ground as the chaos swarms around them.

Just a week earlier some dear pals had helped me move into my new apartment. In a fit of "Gosh-Ain't-it-fun-to-schlep-furniture-up-and-down-43-steps" comedy, we stood on my balcony and threw donut holes across the street. Like cake grenades they bounced and exploded into tiny crumb shrapnel on the sidewalk.... the height of humor through a difficult transition. And now, here were the same dear friends... In another crumby situation, standing their ground and helping me transition again. And then more people came. I thought about what happens in communities in Oklahoma or Kansas when tornadoes strike. Or Florida Hurricanes. Or California Quakes.

It fortified my Hurricane Andrew Theory. When the storm is over and your house is rubble and all former reality gone, you have basically two choices. Become a looter and take advantage of the weak and vulnerable in the neighborhood and grab a stereo through a broken window.... Or become a part of a healing community and help rebuild from the ground up. And now, sitting on my personal heart rubble my loving community members pitched in to help organize a search party for my Spirit. Even the new kids in town, that I may have scowled at because they were the "new kids in town" (sorry) were right there. Unfortunately, some other "trusted old friends" did some emotional looting while I was crying because fear and poverty ate up their humanity. But, Poverty is Poverty and Miracles is Miracles.... And I am beginning to believe that the only viable human emotion is gratitude. That's tougher some days. Oh, by the way, I threw the Magic Princess Ring away. It ran out of magic.... the nature of thin illusions in the face of fat realities. I replaced it immediately with a new magic ju-ju that is working quite well.... Soul Laughter.

Donuts have holes. Foxholes are holes. It is the empty part which makes them what they are and give them meaning. My life has a new hole. I hope this will be part of what makes me meaningful to others in their foxholes.

Survival tips de jour:

1. Please make donations to charities in your community.
2. Suit up and Show up for Community Sponsored Projects.
3. Smile at your neighbors, pet their dogs, ask about their children, give them flowers: Celebrate your belongingness.
4. Beautify your community by adding something or by picking up a bit of litter and tossing it in a trash can.
5. Take your children out for ice cream or for a walk on the beach frequently.
6. If you can't do local politics: at least VOTE !
7. Support your local merchants: buy things at home.
8. Take time to listen... That new person might be a real hero.
9. Commit random acts of community service: Volunteer.
10. Don't miss an opportunity to be present for someone.

(A deep and special thanks to my heart community in Florence, Oregon. Love and ouch, Vali)

Chapter 5

Out the Door

Since I had removed the Magic Princess Ring, I had to walk. Didn't mind. Loved it. In fact, I have actually become addicted to walking, which is an unlikely habit for a former non-movement person. I admit that the transformation began elsewhere. I was at Indiana University, Bloomington, for what I fondly called "Camp PhD"... And I had to walk miles for my food. Talk about your motivation! Heat. Humidity. Tornadoes. I hated it. When I returned home, I felt such relief! All that I had to do was lean over the couch to get to my refrigerator. It then dawned on me that I had been given a rich opportunity. I now call that gift "OTD".... Out The Door! My world is better, richer, and more delightful for the process of going OTD. Walking is indeed a Survival Technique.

Some handy-dandy Definitions:

Walk: (Webster)
To move about in visible form. (Since it doesn't

21

mention feet, those who are in wheelchairs or bedridden can also walk, as long as someone sees them move about!)

Planet: (Dr. Vali)
Webster is a bit unclear on this... So for the sake of discussion, let's agree that it means our cute little Earth.

Please: (Webster)
To have the kindness (please)

Out: (Dr. Vali)
Not in

The: (Dr. Vali)
A handy word

Door: (Webster)
A means of access

For those charming, snowy, sleety, wet, rainy, foggy, windy, drizzled, grey and soggy days of the year when it seems too painful to go OTD, one can indeed find covered shopping malls, bookstores with hardwood floors, large old musty libraries and glaring fluorescent bright markets to move about visibly. On the other hand, if one does brave the realities of wintry weather, the changes of color, muffled sounds, and solitary brilliance of walking become a personal event worthy of being called High Meditation.

It is a holy (wholly) moment to find yourself absolutely alone on a wet and windy beach, not a soul in sight, surrounded by the sounds of grayness. Walk alone on the edge of the continent or on the top of a blown bare hill. The existential components are staggering. The sensuality of feeling all there is to feel at this place of self is the stuff of concerto.

For the more social individual, walking through town, greeting friends and other walkers is gentle soul rhythm. Walking the woods or hills behind your house, sharing a conversation while moseying around the block, or simple greetings at the mailbox are American sonnets waiting to be written. Walking allows you not to miss the violets in the lawn. (Which is different than the violence in the lawn, spoken of by a fearful friend who now fears walking alone in the City of Her Childhood.) We mustn't lose the delights of shoes on concrete, dirt, grass or sand which can instantly become barefoot celebrations when the rain stops. Puddles, once miracles of childhood, still wait for happy feet. Walking in Florence, Oregon's Old Town among the visitors during tourist season is a Mini-Manhattan, and after they leave it is Cape Cod... both are perfect! Walking in Phoenix is to breathe in light. Going OTD in Maui is paradise. Moseying down a dirt road in Cabo San Lucas, BSC, Mexico is to walk through a textbook of culture. Walking barefoot into a dirt field in Kansas is to be Dorothy. At Siletz Bay I walk parallel to a sea lion who swims beside me. We share eye contact thinking our separate thoughts in visible movements. On Port Orford high cliffs I walk above the birds in their visible movements. There is just so much to see and be and walking brings it all back to center. Where do you walk?

I sat once with a dying child in a pediatric hospital. I tried to think how I could entertain or assist her in her "walk through" this hospital stay. She only had mobility in one hand and arm. I gave her a small toy. She grabbed it with glee and created an entire universe on her blanket edge. This little figurine took her OTD via imagination and walked all around her bedside.

Going OTD may mean a walk in the park, or simply finding a "means of access" to your imagination and walking out into the sunlight of your soul.

Whether it is Mind Walkers, Heart Walkers, Country Walkers, Sea Walkers, Sky Walkers, City Walkers, or Soul Walkers... Eye level art and high level heart are accessible to the walking mystic.

Survival tips de jour:

1. Go OTD. Now.
2. If it's raining, put a hanky in your pocket to wipe off eye glasses when they get wet. (So you can't use them as an excuse to stay inside.)
3. Get a map of the best local hikes, trails, walks and parks.
4. Find a walking buddy or a buddy walking.
5. Don't buy special equipment. (Unless it's a really nifty hat. Or two!)
6. Walk to work, school, coffeeshop, church, or store.
7. Offer to walk with a single friend or elderly person, or push someone's wheelchair OTD.
8. Walk for healthy hearts and lean bodies.
9. Walk for charity and for clarity.
10. Walk on the Planet, Please.

Chapter 6

Perfecting the Hang

Perfecting "the hang" is a tricky survival mechanism to which I aspire. So far it is going quite well, but research continues. I look to the experts for guidance, support, encouragement, and mentoring. "Hanging Out" is an essential element of surviving on our planet.

Some handy-dandy Definitions:

Perfect: (Webster)
    Flawless proficiency, something rarely achieved
Perfecting: (Dr. Vali)
    Working at getting something perfect
Hang: (Dr. Vali)
    The fine art of doing as little as possible
Out: (Dr. Vali)
    Anywhere other than where you were when you decided to go Hang
The-Hang: (Dr. Vali)
    The act of consciously participating in perfecting the necessary behaviors, attitudes, philosophies,

wisdoms, postures, gestures and general hoo-haw of doing nothing... And if at all possible getting well paid for doing so

I began comprehending the concept of "The Hang" as a survival element when I was in Grad School. A group of us would meet at the local tavern every Friday afternoon and discuss the illusions and realities of the known and unknown universe. Several of my colleagues would partake in bubbly brews and get good and toasted. I didn't have time to recover from that so I just buzzed over a diet soda. I had kids, housework, homework, a husband... Who had time for a hangover?? On the other hand, without that ritual Hang, I would NEVER have finished school.

Early Hang prerequisites began when I worked in hospitals and clinics where sometimes there is nothing to do but Hang. When one is in a situation where it is clear one has absolutely no control, it is best to just Hang Out. I came to learn that some of the best Hangs were associated with the dying and the birthing processes... Because there isn't anything more honest. So my Hang training has been with scholars, drunks, pregnant mommies, and dying children. From these illustrious experts, I discovered the essence of watching for truth and comedy... Often the same thing. So, my Hang education began early and it continues daily. Every town I have lived in has its own Perfecting the Hang classroom. A favorite cafe, a bench at the park, a driftwood log on a beach, a porch... it doesn't matter. What matters is the process not the geographic location. This is almost a lost art, and it is a very tricky curriculum to perfect. It requires lots of lab hours and much research! Sitting in a favorite booth at a favorite cafe, my feet up on a chair, sun

in my face, diet-soda in my hand, I asked some Hang Experts
– the Masters – for advice and mentoring. They offered a
few tips:

"It's about Relaxation....with two X's." (I guess that
    would be like sleeping with lots of ZZZZ's?)
"Hanging Out is what I do on the Monkey Bars at the
    Playground with my grandbaby."
"Hanging out is about Time. You can Hang for 5
    minutes, 1 hour, or a week. And don't forget the
    'Cyberhang'." (This expert then started a
    dissertation about Einstein's theory of relativity
    and I knew I was in the presence of Hang Genius.)
"One must also consider the 'unhang.'"
"Hanging out is a delicious luxury."
"Directionless conversation and silly philosophizing."
"No schedules, the antithesis of planning."
"Posture is important, and gestures. One must appear
    confident and relaxed, moving very little, yet alert
    in case someone says, 'there are free food samples
    next door' where then you can immediately move
    into Perfecting the Getting Free Food form of
    Hanging out."
"Nothing to do but sit on major rumpage."
"Watch the river go by."

Like the tee-shirt philosopher wrote, "Life isn't short,
it's just that we are dead for so long," The Hang offers
perspective. The only necessary element in The Hang is
you. Just being. Let it go for a few moments. We aren't
running the Universe anyway. I forget that sometimes, unless

I go Hang for awhile. Moving about on top of the planet as we do creates an illusion of separation and difference. When you Hang you may notice that we are all quite similar. The Hang can be open eye meditation or sentient siesta. Find a bench. Watch the world go by. You have a free ticket to the best seat in the Universe... Your unique perception of reality.

Survival tips de jour:

1. Hang near a river and watch it roll.
2. Hang by a Garden: Do The Hang with dirt and seeds, and weeds. (Flowers are organized weeds while weeds have perfected The Hang. Don't kill all of them just because they aren't following your agenda!)
3. Hang by the ocean. Watch the tide change. Twice.
4. Hang on a curb and pretend the people going past are the parade.
5. Teach an overworked friend how to Hang Out.
6. If you get down and feel like Hanging it up, Hang on, and go Hang Out.
7. If you can't allow yourself time to do nothing, take time to do little.
8. Try The Hang in five-minute segments until it feels natural. (If it lasts more than six months, perhaps you should work on the Unhang.)
9. Recall the elegance of childhood: meaningless activities which created meaning.
10. Don't just look, see. Don't just exist, be!

Chapter 7

Poly wah-wah

Would anyone like to help me murder Pollyanna? She's starting to really get on my nerves. Rah, Rah, Rah...life is great, keep a chipper attitude, soul survivor, life's a dream-sha-boom, grey skies are gonna clear up put on a happy face, once there was a little old ant tried to move a rubber tree plant, success means getting up one more time than you fall down, and have a nice day. Makes me want to puke...how about you? I think it is very important to survival to take a moment now and then to wallow in the poor-me's of life and give it enough credence so that you can then again return to gratitude and joy as a choice not a performance. So take off the Magic Princess Ring and pull up a pity pot.

Some handy-dandy Definitions:

Pollyanna: (Disney)
A wonderful film by Walt Disney about a young girl who finds gladness in everything

Chipper: (Dr. Vali)
A happy attitude that says life is all good
Reality: (Dr. Vali)
Sometimes the opposite of chipper

I was writing this wonderful upbeat commentary about my recent vacation to Mexico. You know – tan, music, dancing until dawn with my adorable husband, the turquoise Sea of Cortez, pelicans skimming over the Pacific.....the whole glorious works. Then the Red Cross called me to do my Dr. Vali thing because weather disasters had just destroyed and devastated a bunch of lives and I was more than glad to help and I was trying to stay chipper and remember my vacation and I couldn't in the face of such pain and loss and rah-rah-rah-rah.....**who cares**?

Life sucks. Let's just face it, finally and at last. How many times can a person put on a plastic smile and sing the verse from Annie, "The sun will come out tomorrow" without sitting in a heap of sorrow and pointing to the mess?

Sometimes it is essential to take time off from the happily ever after and weep over the losses. This does not mean move your furniture into the region of pity, but set aside a time for it. Perhaps it should be a national holiday.

I am ready to declare a **NATIONAL VICTIMS DAY**. I think Hallmark is missing a major commercial bet here. I visualize a national holiday where people still have to go to work, but they don't get paid for it. I'm planning on dressing in black. I will be wearing long elbow length gloves and dark sunglasses under the veil on my hat. I will go to a public place, lie down, have someone draw a chalk mark around my body and place a donation hat for people to toss their quarters. I will demand that people bring me casseroles. I will sing the blues on a street corner. I will drag my tragic countenance through the mall and insist that people HEAR ME!!!!! It just isn't possible to release the Inner Victim until someone hears it scream, "WHAT ABOUT ME!!!!!!"

And until that voice is heard by a truly sympathetic ear and heart, the voice gets louder and louder and louder... Even if that loudness is disguised in silence and passivity. And how can desperate victims listen to victims when they are shouting OUCH at the top of their collective lungs... And everyone has a boo-boo.

So, to hellwithit....let's just give in to the urge to purge and gather around the bucket and share the pain. Misery loves company, and if I have to write a chipper word today I'll feel like an idiot. Because when you are really and truly bleeding from the eyes, words don't matter at all.

I am a world class survivor, and I know what it takes to get the job done.... choosing Faith over Fear.... ALWAYS! So today, I'm not going to be fearful of my desperate Inner Victim, and instead take the poor whiny girl out for lunch. Want to join us? Oh, just leave me alone, go away...who needs you! Have a nice day.

Survival tips de jour:

1. Pain creates temporary tunnel vision and self centered behavior...it's called survival.
2. Pain is nature's way of telling us something isn't quite correct.
3. Have a good supply of cartoon character bandaids in your medicine chest for your boo-boos.
4. Give up.
5. Start over.
6. Don't collect boo-boos like beads on a bracelet.
7. Grieve publicly so others can know that it is OKAY to feel bad once in a while... That is reality too.
8. Helping another victim is a way out of your pain, but not a substitute for feeling and healing your own.
9. Look in the mirror and tell yourself how brave you are, and know that I know you are brave also.
10. Crying is part of recovering.

Chapter 8

Isn't It Romantic?

Roses are red, violets are blue... Romance is ready, are you? This is a perfect time to write about romance. I just ended a memorable one and can reflect upon the notion without passion or prejudice, and in fact, be completely unbiased and neutral. After researching the topic dispassionately with a number of friends, it seems that romance remains a mystery. Like sleep it is somehow essential, leads to dreams and yet remains resistant to simple description. Romance is both noun and verb, suggesting form and function. Is it science or art? Biological or spiritual? Can romance exist in a vacuum? Considering the gravity of falling in love, what are the quantum mechanics of romance?

Some handy-dandy Definitions:

Romance: (Webster)
A medieval verse, something that lacks basis in fact, an emotional attraction, a passionate love affair, a language

Romance: (Dr. Vali) Ahhhhhhhhhh

Apparently the "R Word" can be dangerous. Last week I sent a seasoned romantic in New York a greeting card which depicted an innocent in a white suit, holding a bouquet of flowers stepping smilingly off a cliff. Below were countless toothful wolves with open mouths. The caption read, "A romantic enters the world."

If romance is a risky leap off a cliff then poetry is the bungee cord. I adore writing romantic poetic verse on airport cafe napkins. So, what makes us leap into a romance? Dreams? Memories? Goals? Fantasies? Perhaps it's a primal mating behavior based on our mammalian ancestors. Or maybe it comes from memories of your own recent past. Do you recall that time a long time ago when a loved one carved I LOVE YOU out of celery sticks on a first picnic. Who was it that sent you those surprise roses? Romance is love notes, halves of theatre tickets, finding a true heart because of a tornado, exiting the theater after Dr. Zhivago to walk home through newly fallen snow, the smile in his eyes over the mask in the delivery room that even an ancient divorce can't fade, midnight phone calls to share dreams, a coat tossed over your shoulders in the rain, remembered anniversaries, and long forgotten lyrics. Romance is anything that you define as romantic.

Romance is sweet. Tender. It's about coming together. Romance: the sweet bread crumbs which attract the birds and bees. But what is it? Is it sitting and watching your millionth sunset with the same partner? Or a first glance across a crowded room? A hope? A miracle? A belief that there is union in the universe? A dazzling glimpse at the

34

face of God? Buddha seeing Buddha? The reality of oneness in a separatists universe? A movie with popcorn? Comedy? A carnival-won teddy bear? A belief system dependent upon group agreement? The "do you remember when's" of tomorrows? The glue which holds a relationship together? (Happily-ever-after-epoxy?) A fleeting moment? A mood? A first kiss? A Sondheim musical? Writing initials in wet sand? Dancing cheek to cheek? A Bogie movie? TV dinners by candlelight? La Boheme? A tipped hat, a door opened? What is it? Is it essential? Is life worth anything without it? What is it to you? Are you addicted? Shall we all gather at Romance Anonymous Meetings? Is it a drug that is too good to give up?

Hello.

My name is Vali.

I'm a Romance Junkie.

(Sigh.)

Survival tips de jour:

1. Go dancing anyway.
2. Leave a love note in a fun place.
3. Paste candy on paper in the shape of a heart and put it in someone's briefcase or under their pillow.
4. Believe.
5. Reinvent Gratitude daily, act "as if" you are in love.
6. Recognize Romance even when it doesn't look like it does on Television or movies.
7. Be the person you want that other person to be like.
8. Write poetry by candlelight... Even if no one else ever reads it.
9. Put Christmas lights up in your bedroom... It's like being on a cruise ship.
10. Find a romantic gift that only costs a dollar. I bet it will become a most favorite treasure if it comes from your heart.

Chapter 9

Lucky Old Sun

Life is just so difficult. Challenges and travails and in fact, I'm writing this chapter from deep behind the war torn trenches of, of.... Well... No. I'm up to my armpits in alligators and I must... Well, actually I am writing these words from a warm beach in Maui. It's tough duty, but someone has to do it. The Magic Princess Ring has now been replaced with a little silver toe ring – the Magic Toe Ring – which is currently on my foot smoodgied in the warm sand. The sun is pink and oranging itself into the sea. I'm facing west. Sunsets, an important part of survival.

Some handy-dandy Definitions:

Sunset: (Webster)
    A period of decline

Jaded: (Webster)
    Dulled by excess

Bill: (Dr. Vali)
The name of one of my cats

Red sky at night, sailors delight. Red sky at morning, sailors take warning. This little analogy actually works and can be used to predict picnics. Sunsets are, in fact, the apparent descent of the sun below the horizon with accompanying atmospheric effects as the time when the upper limb of the sun disappears below the sensible horizon as a result of the diurnal rotation of the earth...RIGHT! As though someone in love cares!!! Red sails in the sunset or 77 Sunset Strip, sunsets are sunrises inside out, endings on our hemisphere are beginnings elsewhere. I saw the sun explode in the sea, it burst in glorious majesty...and in the misty magic morn, I saw that golden sun reborn. Rebirth has always been a symbol with the sunrise, and sunsets have been associated with age and transition. However, if you think of it, the sun doesn't really set.... It just keeps rolling around the earth....the true center of the Universe!!! (Is that working for you?) So the sun, that pesky bright ball of light and hope above our planet, be it at rise or set, is an important metaphor... So important that it might even be a metafive.

I'm not overwhelmed with Maui sunsets. Just whelmed. It's not that they aren't swell, it's just that they are remarkably like sunsets at other places with palm trees. I'm so jaded by my own wonderful life that I began to brag to the Maui locals about what they were missing. A few folks got dreamy-eyed and sighed remembering honeymoons or trips they had taken to Oregon or California or Japan. Yawning nonchalantly behind my hand I said, "Wow, nice sunset."

38

I grew up envious of people who got to go to Hawaii, like that was the end of the known universe. I really enjoy our Aloha state, but I have discovered that a sunset in Seattle or Kansas is just as amazing if my mind is in the right place....and that is not a geographic location. So, I suggest that the next time you hear the neighbors are off to Maui, or off to a cruise to the Caribbean or Tahiti, wish them a cheery and un-envious ta-ta, and then go catch the Sunset on your porch. I am grateful beyond belief that I get to travel, but just like Dorothy said, "There's no place like home...." It's great to be jaded!

Survival tips de jour:

1. Never let the sun set on your anger.
2. Call Somerset Maughm "Sunset Mom" just to bug your literary friends.
3. Watch sunset from any bridge in your community.
4. Try to suck a lifesaver or a piece of Salt Water Taffy all the way through your next sunset.
5. Go to a park and hold hands through a sunset with your lover.
6. Propose during a sunset.
7. Do a yoga sun salutation on the beach at sunset.
8. Grab a notebook and pen and write poetry about sunset colors, or sunset sounds.
9. Learn all the verses to "Sunrise-Sunset" from Fiddler on the Roof and sing them with gusto. (And if gusto isn't available sing with a friend.)
10. Join other Sunset-Pilgrims who find their own special spot to catch the release of today into the colorful arms of tomorrow.

Chapter 10

Passion

"What is my passion?" I asked myself passionately. Without a passion there is no energy to survive the daily grind of life. So many people think passion has to do with boy meets girl kind of stuff. That is such a small reflection of passion that it is like describing the sky as a blue place. Finding and honoring your passion is an essential survival tip because a passionless life is no way to survive.

Some Handy Dandy definitions

Passion: (Webster)
The sufferings of Christ between the night of the Last Supper and his death, an oratorio based on the gospel, suffering, the state or capacity of being acted on by external agents or forces, the emotions as distinguished from reason, violent, intense or overmastering feeling, ardent affection, a strong devotion to some activity, object or concept

Passion: (Dr. Vali)
The reason we want to get out of bed each day to give something back to the universe

I have a passion for survival. And although Webster included suffering in his definition of passion, I perceive passion as a way to eliminate the suffering. My definition of passion includes giving something back to the universe.

I have met people who profess a passion for something, like cocaine use or bungee jumping. I suspect sometimes there is a fine line between passion and addiction. I know people who are addicted to suffering and passionately try to get others to join them in their misery. No thanks. My RSVP to that invitation will read, "Oh, gee, thanks for the invitation but I have other plans."

I have found that there are people in this world who fear passion. They keep it away from every corner of their lives except the bedroom. These are the folks who do not go and dance in the wind because it might disrupt their hairdo. They miss the passionate voice of the wind explaining the secrets of the trees. They are the ones who don't stick their toes in the river and miss the brrrrrrrrrrr and call of ancient deep water songs. They don't go shopping for candy canes on Christmas Eve because of the crowds and miss the silliness and whimsy. They don't use big voices or laugh out loud because they must control their impulses and miss the bubbles of giggles and random hurrahs. They don't try creating art because they haven't had a class in it and they don't draw outside the lines and never scribble in the margins of their books. I doubt if they ever put a rhubarb leaf over their head as an umbrella or slept with a teddy bear as an adult. I wonder if they could cry big tears at a cheesy movie or write a love song. It takes a lot of faith to do these things. I often forget that the word passion is associated with the story of Christ's walk to death which was based on His faith and not His fear. Passion has to do with the energy it takes to do something about our faith, to act on it not just to hang around believing in it. A dancer has passion when he commits his tired feet to his shoes and his old shoes to the wooden rehearsal floor and his hungry ear to the music and his longing heart to the movement. A mother has passion as she gets up in the middle of the night without anger to clean up the mess from a sick baby and still takes time to hum the lullaby. A father has passion when he doesn't give up on parenting even though the divorce has made it necessary to climb a mountain of faith every time he wants to visit with his children. A child shows passion with a little hand that reaches out. An artist shows passion when she does her art in spite of all the commercial elements against it. A sweeper shows passion when he sweeps knowing it matters to remove the chaos and that someone with passion will notice the difference.

People show passion when they suit up and show up, speak up and commit action. Passion isn't about the empty words, "How are you"? Passion is the fullness of words like, "How can I help?" Passion can include showing compassion. It is no mistake the word Compassion holds the word passion in its arms. Compassion is the action of feeling something worthy and doing something about it. Passion is singing on top of a hill in a loud voice and whispering to a violet in a meadow. It is not just thinking or saying, it is doing – doing your art, whatever it is. Passion is more than blustering words. Passion can be silent and end in mighty works done anonymously. Passion adds dimension to the flatness of life.

Passion can be dusting the furniture or emptying the garbage in the right spirit. Passion can be great art or great heart. If life was the ocean, passion would be the waves. If life was the sky, passion would be the bigness of it. If life was you, passion would be your soulwork.

Tips De Jour

1. Find your passion.
2. Live and Act upon your passion.
3. Honor the passions of others.
4. Eat passion fruit.
5. Attend a passion play.
6. Play passionately.
7. Put the passion back into compassion.
8. Act on faith not fear.
9. Use passion to make a difference.
10. See number 1 and then refer to number 2.

Chapter 11

Spare Me

What a long year this month has been! There is only one thing that I can possibly do to survive the rest of this month....I'm going bowling! Bowling, an important survival tool.

Some handy-dandy Definitions:

Bowling: (Don Johnson, PBA Hall of Famer)
   The most popular leisure time sport in the USA.
   Second only to fishing.

Fishing: (Dr. Vali)
   What many people live for

In 1916, a 3 bedroom house sold for about $2700, a new Ford for about $350. The average annual income was about $806 and Betty Grable and Olivia de Havilland were born. 1916 was the official year that women's bowling began. I started this September. Now, when I was a little one, my brother told me that thunder was just God's Angels Bowling in Heaven.... no wonder bowling scared me. I am trying to overcome my bias.

I once thought that the most important part of bowling was the readily available health food. **MMMMMMM**... Melted cheese product over stale nacho chips, beer, popcorn, and a dollar's worth of pickles and chocolate. Serious gourmet!

And then there is the Fashion? Just try to top those snappy 2-tone shoes!

A non-bowling friend reminded me of all the available fresh air and someone else mentioned the values of aerobic exercise! Food, fashion, fresh air, exercise and amazing psychological motivation. Where else can one participate in such grand excitement for a little "X" or a little " /" on a piece of paper? As a PhD type of person, I am frighteningly motivated by little cosmic report cards of one sort or another and it seems that bowling scores qualify! Ah, yes... roll a ball down a wooden floor, hear a wonderful grumpling-thumpling sound, wait in hopeful expectation, and get instant gratification. Life is good.

Apparently, based on external feedback, I have become rowdy. Our team's motto is "we bowl to be annoying!" I have discovered that bowling is quite cathartic. I can bowl out my anger, bowl out my angst, bowl out my memories, my grief, my hopes, my fears, my pain, and my comedy. I can bowl out my heart and soul while surrounded by other bowling pals.

Bowling is a great survival tip. On a cold-and-bleak-wintery-Sunday evening the sidewalks may be rolled up

46

and the malls closed. The movies may be boring and your friends have gone to Mexico for the sun. If you go to the beach you find that even the seagulls have gone to the bowling alley parking lot. Fortunately, there is a place to go. There exists a busy-bright-noisy place filled with energy that can perk up the most cynical couch potato..... trust me. I have had a rough and painful winter, and if it wasn't for bowling, it would have been much, much harder to wait for spring. Maybe it is where Angels Make Thunder. And, if you don't want to bowl, go for the food!

Survival tips de jour:

1. Go bowling. It will be okay.
2. Go watch someone bowl. Yell loudly using bowling terms like:
   "Knock down those maples!" Or,
   "Go get 'em keglers!"
3. Watch bowling at home. Yell bowling terms at the TV set.
4. Go to the bowling alley for dinner. (But have pizza delivered.)
5. Support your favorite charity by creating a bowl-a-thon.
6. Buy used bowling shirts at a thrift store to look cool.
7. Don't make fun of bowling anymore. It's really a good thing.
8. If you bowl right handed always eat the popcorn with the left hand.
9. If you bowl left handed always eat the popcorn with the right hand.
10. Bowl someone over with an invitation to go Bowling.

Chapter 12

The 6 Stages of Waiting

My Magic Ring isn't working, and I feel sick. I'm waiting at the doctor's office. Whereas hanging out is an art form, waiting is just obnoxious.

Some handy-dandy Definitions:

Waiting: (Webster)
    Staying in place with expectation
Waiting: (Dr. Vali)
    Obnoxious, tedious, agitating anguish which can turn a regular person into a maniac
Waiting: (Dr. Vali)
    An unexpected and unplanned opportunity for spiritual development

I am delighted to report that survival, which often depends upon the art of waiting, has just reached a new epoch by my discovery of the SIX (count 'em, 6) STAGES OF WAITING AT THE DOCTOR'S OFFICE. Elizabeth Kübler Ross thinks she's so cool with her 5 stages of grieving (Denial, Bargaining, Anger, Depression and Acceptance). She may be smug now, but just wait until she hears about this...

STAGE ONE: Anticipation

This stage is marked by certain activities, such as, but not limited to: checking your watch, flipping through magazines (tearing out recipes suggests a need for immediate professional intervention), generally fantasizing that any moment you will be next.

(I suppose this may slightly resemble the Denial stage if you actually believe that your appointment will be on time.)

STAGE TWO: Reality Testing

You ask the receptionist if her watch and office clock match your watch. You have now typically gone through all the magazines (even Field and Stream), made a grocery list, and paced to the water fountain. Extreme cases find some calling CORRECT TIME on the pay phone or asking the receptionist what was the "exact time" of your appointment.

(The Bargaining stage is close if you believe your hints might actually effect change.)

STAGE THREE: Cranky and Puny

You realize that if you stay you have been exploited once again by the mindless elite classist system of the Flexner

Model of American Medicine. If you storm out you will have to wait for another 3 weeks for an appointment and still feel puny. You have discovered that pacing and hinting are as useless as the magazines which are old and have been handled by people with diseases of unknown etiologies. You ruminate that you could have been a doctor yourself if it hadn't been for_____(fill in the blank).

(Similar to the Anger stage, because.... Well, you figure it out, because the receptionist looked at me and I think it's my turn to see the Doc...)

(Apparently not.)

(Crank. Sniff.)

STAGE FOUR: Life Stinks

It's Monday, you feel puny, everyone else on the planet is fine, your life lacks meaning, and suddenly that article in the women's magazine looks appealing – "How to change your life completely in just 15 minutes." (If you worry about having time to finish reading it along with the original text of War and Peace translated into Danish, see Stage Two.)

(Like the Depression stage, similar to the Crash of the 1920's, only much longer.)

STAGE FIVE: Whatever

You settle in, put your feet up, begin to counsel other people in earlier stages of waiting, advise the receptionist as to newly arrived patients, work on a writing project or doodle new house plans on the back of a "How to Manage Asthma" brochure, wave to the nurse as she calls in other patients, play with the chewed up kiddy toys, reorganize magazines in alphabetical order, and are a bit annoyed when (if) finally called.

STAGE SIX: Deja Vu Here We Go Again

Being called into the "Inner Sanctum" doesn't mean you are going to see the doctor immediately... now does it?

Survival tips de jour:

1.   Wait.
2-10.   Well that probably says it all.

Chapter 13

For the Birds

I'm swimming in the Sea of Cortez, off the Baja peninsula, watching the Whales make their U-turn back to Oregon...great place....warm water...smart whales. A huge pelican lands nearby and although whales are amazing, I am reminded that birds are essential to survival.

Some handy-dandy Definitions:

Bird: (Webster)
   Any of a class of warm blooded vertebrates distinguished by having the body more or less completely covered with feathers and the forelimbs modified as wings
The Birds: (Dr. Vali)
   A scary movie by Alfred Hitchcock

Birdman of Alcatraz: (Dr. Vali)
   A movie about a scary criminal
Bye-Bye Birdie: (Dr. Vali)
   Another scary movie if you really think about it
Larry Bird: (Dr. Vali)
   A brilliant athlete who scares less brilliant athletes
Lady Bird: (Dr. Vali)
   A former President's wife
Birder: (Webster)
   One who birds

The Magic Princess Ring, which was replaced by a Magic Toe Ring in Maui, has now been amazingly replaced by the **Diamond of Truth Ring**...which instantly transported me to Cabo San Lucas for a delicious honeymoon... How precious it is to have a miracle after a series of catastrophes.... may the LIGHT always bridge the darkness!! In all honesty Light seemed easier to see in Mexico and from the 11th floor of the Disneyland Hotel than in the dim West Coast rains of "Febrrrrrrrrruary".

Generally the coastlines all along the Pacific Rim aren't that much different than the coastline of Oregon. (Okay, add a few palm trees!) But the Maui coastline looks like Yachats, Oregon and the Baja Peninsula looks like the Tri-Cities, Washington and gee, Cabo San Lucas is essentially Oregon with Mexican food. (Okay... Really great Mexican food.) I search for common denominators. People all smile in the same language and I haven't been anywhere there hasn't been diet soda available... yet. And Birds.

Birds are everywhere. Sometimes birds are not appreciated because of their annoying tendency to gift your

54

hat. But those feathery pals are a miracle of variety, simplicity, colors, shapes, sizes and skills the likes of which are phenomenal. I was taken by the nonchalant pelicans in Cabo San Lucas. They were as casual and plentiful as your basic coastal seagull. Of course, any real local coast person knows that not all gulls are sea gulls. There are land gulls, car gulls, grocery store gulls, roof gulls, resort hotel balcony gulls, parking lot gulls, and garbage dump gulls.

Have you ever noticed those little brown itsy bitsy whatchamacallit birds that seem to be universal? My sweetie and I had some fly into our Mexican Villa for an early honeymoon breakfast. Those cuties just tickled us as we tossed them crumbs from our feast. We had scored one of those 3-story-Architectural Digest-glorious-overlooking-the-sea-and-make-your-friends-very-envious-rose-petals-and-mosquito-nets-and-chocolates-on-the-pillows-and-three-extra-beds suites, and we were gifted one morning with little birdies flying through the kitchen looking for bits of Mexican pastries. Very Cute. My daughter has always called them "McDonald Birds" since they gather near tossed french fries.

Later, at the Disneyland Hotel...an-elegant-11th floor-concierge-suite-overlooking-our-favorite-theme-park-yeah-chocolates-on-the-pillows place, I decided to take a little siesta to give Mr. Wonderful an opportunity to go buy me presents. I hear this coota-coo-coota-coo....coota-coota-coo...and open my eyes to see our elegant room filled with a herd (pod?) (school?) of pigeons. I shooed them out gently (in case they were Disney fake animated birds). Later that day, in the Tiki-Room, the birds were eerily realistic. In fact, they were real enough that when these birds asked the audience to sing along we all obeyed mindlessly. Thank goodness they didn't instruct us to go do evil deeds. Anyhow, even the Lion King Parade, a tear-producing-miracle-of-sound-energy-soul-dance sort of production ended with the performers releasing white doves into the crowd. Wonderful! Everywhere we went birds offered little feathered blessings of light, fun, silliness, mystery and twinkle.

Waking up to bird songs wherever we landed was music to our tired traveler ears. When one is a very, very long way from home in a foreign country, it is comforting to hear a familiar language...birdsongs. A very elderly Native American Medicine Woman once invested in my heart. She gifted me with the understanding of bird talk, a precious way to pay attention...and as I now hear the crows outside my studio door they remind me to remind you that without birds there would have been no dreams of flight. Ecologically alone, the chain of food which balances our planetary survival is more dependent upon the birds than most folks know. The expression "it's for the birds" has more meaning than you'd suspect. If the birdies don't eat the bugs which eat the other bugs which eat the leaves which make the oxygen which eats the carbon dioxide we would soon be in deep planetary guacamole.

What a surprise that a bunch of birds made such an impression at such major places as a glorious Mexican Honeymoon, and Disneyland..... Sometimes it's easy to focus on the Big Stars, while it's the little backstage pals, who work for birdseed, that keep the show going.

Survival tips de jour:

1. Feed the birds, tuppence a bag.
2. Find ways to kill your garden bugs which will not throw off the food chain.
3. Don't use bird feathers in craft projects if it kills birds.
4. Support bird watching, or injured waterfowl rescue projects.
5. Close your eyes and listen to the calls of the Canada Geese as they fly by.
6. Keep your cats well fed with commercial cat food.
7. Please don't wear those goofy baseball caps covered with fake bird doo-doo. (ICK.)
8. Go to the library or bookstore or pet store and learn more about birds.
9. Cross stitch "A bird in the hand is worth two in the bush," and give it away (quickly).
10. Take time to listen to the birds sing in the morning.

Chapter 14

Water Water Everywhere

I suppose you already know that all the water that exists on the Planet is already here. Oh, it moves around a bit, from ocean to clouds, to river to sinks...but all that has existed or will ever exist now exists. Kind of makes me think about water once in a while. Water, an important part of Survival.

Some handy-dandy Definitions:

Water: (Dr. Vali)
   What don't you understand about water?
Ocean: (Dr. Vali)
   What don't you understand about water?

I spent most of my happy childhood vacations at the Pacific Ocean. I knew that someday I would have to be at sea-level to be a happy grown-up lady. What's really weird is that after all the years I lived on the water I haven't been boating very often. Recently I got a cruise on a tug boat and a pirate vessel. Highways look different from the water. Water looks different from the water. Things move at a different pace, and there is a sense of humility present in the vulnerability of being off land. Water is magic. Water is scary. Water makes up a really large percentage of our bodies. What happens to body water when the tide changes? 2 parts hydrogen, and 1 part oxygen equals water. Sort of like a fluid oreo cookie, right? How much water is in watermelon? Watercress? Water buffalo? Waterloo?

The magic of water is that it changes form and shape, and becomes different critters. Water becomes a luxurious hot tub event, and then it becomes a dangerous drive in the fog. Water is the stuff of intravenous fluids keeping a friend alive or the ice which gets a car out of control and kills a friend on a winter night. Water is fought for in the desert and sneered at by tourists with short vacations and picnickers. It is too absent in a drought in Africa and too plentiful in a Midwest flood zone. Water is life and death and comes in glass containers filled with pretty bubbles. It is necessary for tides and slides, clouds and fish. You get it in gushes and drips and sometimes a crystal finger dish. Rainbows and sunsets are nothing without water....so I guess water is necessary for romance. It is hard to have a regular birthday cake without water. And where would the Coast Guard be without it? Or an Olympic Swim Team. Or mud. Or a bubble bath. As a friend of mine wrote: "Water, water everywhere, it makes you stop and think. That only water clear and clean is good enough to drink." And although people keep telling me I "should" drink 8 glasses a day...I refuse, because water is so darn, well, you know...watery.

Baptisms or showers, go water your flowers... splashing it around blesses the Universe and the Universe gives back puddles for barefeet.

Survival tips de jour

1. Drink 8 glasses a day.
2. Fix leaky sinks and drips.
3. Be careful where you dispose of icky things, it might kill the water forever.
4. Go on a river or lake or ocean in a boat...don't wait, invite yourself.
5. Wade in a river and skip stones across a lake.
6. Ask yourself, "How many drops does a dew drop drop if a dew drop does drop dew?
7. Bless the rains when they come, even if it ruins your picnic.
8. Save a bucket of rainwater to shampoo your hair.
9. Say thank you to the water as you shower or bathe.
10. Write a thank you note or say thanks to a firefighter, a lifeguard, or a Coast Guard person.

Chapter 15

Give Sand a Chance

The universe is full of such fun things to write about. Recently I went to eastern Washington State. I heard someone call it the Sand Capitol of the World. How silly. Obviously they had never been to the Pacific Ocean on a windy day. Let's hear it for sand....an essential survival element of our planet:

Some Handy-Dandy Sandy Definitions:

Sand: (Webster)
A loose granular material resulting from the disintegration of rocks that is used in mortar, glass, abrasives and foundry molds.

Sand: (Dr. Vali)
See inside your shoes at the beach

Dirt: (Dr. Vali)
Big sand

Gravel: (Dr. Vali)
Really big sand

Sand. Sand. Sand. Grits in your teeth and runs through your hand. It smooshes through your toes wherever you stand becoming part of your picnic that you never planned. A waiter was pouring my coffee, and I looked past him out the windows and saw the Columbia River and its surrounding sandy-tumbleweedy banks. Desert. I survived living in Arizona by pretending it was a very (V-E-R-Y) long sandy beach. I swam joyfully in the Colorado River thinking of all the flecks of ancient sand that had been carried from the gorges of the Grand Canyon. The Columbia River carries sand too. Rivers do that, carry sand and such from place to place. I move around a lot myself. So does sand. Dirt doesn't have such an adventurous life. Dirt stays home and has a bad reputation. Gossip is called "dirt" and is used by people who don't get around enough to have an adventurous life so they talk about each other.

I took a trip inland one afternoon. I had been too long on the coast and got excited when I saw dirt. You know, soil-potted-plant-stuff-humus-squeeze-it-together-in-your-hand-while-you're-planting-a-garden-dirt. One doesn't see much dirt when one lives on the sandy shores of the Pacific. Some folks try to get rid of dirt.... Coast folks actually order it from dirt catalogues. Hard to do a garden in sand...unless you adore beach grass. But in an aesthetic sense, sand is more fun than dirt. Compare the following list to see if you agree:

62

Sand box	Dirt box
Sandstone	Dirt stone
Sand in hour glasses	Dirt in hour glasses
Sand dunes	Dirt dunes
Sandee Dee	Dirty Dee
Sandy (Annie's dog)	Dirty (our dog)
Sand paintings	Dirt paintings
Sand Castles	Dirt Castles
George Sand	George Dirt
The Sandman	The Dirtman
Sandles	Dirtles
Sandpaper	Dirtpaper

All we are saying, is give sand a chance.... My family moved when I was a wee one. My biggest loss (next to my position as the resident triangle genius in the kindergarten rhythm band) was the sand box at my day care. I missed my sandbox so much that Mom made me a sand tray while Daddy built a sand box. 25 years later I discovered that Sand Play is one of the most powerful and useful and helpful of all the Child Psychology Therapies. 30 years later I met a brilliant woman in Graduate school. We discovered an instant affection and professional regard for one another. We later discovered we had played in that same wonderful daycare sandbox. We both have PhD's and work as Mental Health Counselors. Hmmm. Must have been the sand.

Sand is neat, sand is convenient, sand is happy. Sand. Cuter than dirt.

Survival tips de jour

1. Don't get mad at sand.
2. Make a sandbox for a child or yourself.
3. Make barefoot prints or write your lover's initials on the beach.
4. Make a sand castle.
5. Do something nice for sand....don't litter.
6. Learn the words to "Mr. Sandman" and sing along with friends.
7. Remember what the cat said on Christmas Eve when it came back from a walk on the shore....... "I have Sandy Claws."
8. Write a research grant to study sand. Travel to places with sand, such as, but not limited to :
Gold Beach, Oregon
Aberdeen, Washington
Santa Monica, California
Maui, Hawaii
Saudi Arabia, Saudi Arabia
Jamaica, Jamaica
Oklahoma, Oklahoma
Cabo San Lucas, BCS, Mexico
Bali (sigh)
9. Sand something.
10. Honor the drifts in the sand, and the drifts in your life.

Chapter 16

Bricks

My new patio deck just became my metaphor de-jour. Granted, I'm the kind of person who can make a metaphor out of anything. (Go ahead and ask me about my Tapioca Theory sometime.) Nonetheless, Dave and I just rebuilt our patio. We built the deck so we could sit under the shade tree and drink diet soda and contemplate the Universe.

Some handy-dandy Definitions:

Brick: (Webster)
> A handy sized unit of building or paving material typically of moist clay hardened by heat, a good fellow, a rectangular compressed mass

Brick: (Dr. Vali)
> The little red cubes of earth miracles that my daughter the mason used in her work of making fireplaces for Santa

Project: (Dr. Vali)
A clever little idea that turns into the reinvention of civilization

The project started with a sweet little idea I had about getting 10 or 20 bricks to surround a tree. Kablooey, the cute became logarithmic and a project was born. We hauled 870 bricks. At the beginning I could carry 2 at a time, now I can carry 8. The old deck was rotten underneath and as we pulled up the wood, the lumber oozed from years of neglect. We schlepped rotten parts and tossed them over the fence. We smoothed the earth. We hauled 3 yards of gravel and 2 yards of sand, packed it down with a nifty earth compactor machine we rented, placed the bricks and had a bar-b-que. HA! Like it would be a metaphor if it was that easy? (A good life metaphor requires grit.)

Actually what happened was more like this: We worked and got sweaty, we bled from injuries and fought, we laughed until we fell down in the heat, we got frustrated and didn't speak, we hugged and tickled and then ignored each other, we giggled at how silly it was for us to try to be engineers, we wretched and twitched and hauled heavy loads, we pushed our capacities beyond our previously known limitations, we swore and we sang....and that was just the first 15 minutes! At the end, we set the bricks in place, squeezing them into spaces they didn't want to go. We wiggled them and redid entire rows to accumulate 1/118th of an inch of space so these old bricks could fit into their new home. These weren't new bricks. Used. They were bricks with a story. A history. Already been through a lot. They were removed from an old warehouse one at a time, brick by brick, washed by hand, and none of them matched. Lovely and glorious old bits of our planet. Not typical. More like an ancient road in Mexico.

At the last gap we stopped to contemplate the moment. In it we placed the ugliest most uneven brick to remind us of shadow, pain, anger, fear and our bravery and persistence. Our deck is perfect in its imperfection. It's a lot like us. Charming. Bumpy. Glorious. Uneven. Unique. Old. A sanctuary of early morning peace. Each time we look at it we hug. It's hard to work with another person. But one of us kept the vision in mind when the other forgot. I can barely imagine what bravery it will take to build world peace, brick by brick. Flexibility isn't easy. Bricks and people don't bend easily. Perhaps when people or nations war it is because they lost the vision of the sanctuary of peace they wanted in the first place. Or they just didn't have enough tapioca!

Survival tips de jour

1. Beware of small ideas, they sometimes turn into great visions.
2. Build your dreams brick by brick, and try to be flexible.
3. Do something you can't do.
4. Recycle bricks and other neat stuff.
5. Instead of going to an expensive health spa, use bricks or 2-pound bags of dried beans to lift weights.
6. When life turns tricky, use a metaphor to give it meaning.
7. Sit on the porch or patio with someone you love .
8. When healing a relationship, start at the foundation and work up.
9. Contemplate your smallest achievements.
10. Hug a mason and thank them for all they create.

Chapter 17

The Sky

Twinkle, Twinkle, Little Star, How I wonder what you are!! Recent wanderings make me question who is running the sky.

Some handy-dandy Definitions:

God: (Dr. Vali)
> God

Disney: (Dr. Vali)
> Walt, an original genius of creativity and good timing

Speilberg: (Dr. Vali)
> Steven, another original genius of creativity and good timing

Wayne Newton: (His Publicity Team)
> Mr. Las Vegas

Extra-terrestrials: (Dr. Vali)
> A discussion which would take much too much time to get into here and now, but if you buy me a

cup of coffee I'd be glad to have a very detailed
discussion about my theories
NASA: (Their Publicity Team)
The National Aeronautics and Space
Administration
Sky: (Webster)
The upper atmosphere that constitutes an
apparent great vault or arch over the earth
Sky: (Dr. Vali)
Look up. Big. Pretty. Wow.
Cloud: (Webster)
Visible mass of particles of water or ice in the
form of fog, mist, or haze suspended at a
considerable height in the air, a light filmy, puffy,
or billowy mass seeming to float in the air
Cloud: (Dr. Vali)
Look up. Big. Pretty. Wow.
Cloud: (Disney's Pooh)
"Tutt-tutt, looks like rain."

SHOPPING MALL, LAS VEGAS, NEVADA: A mall
that plays tricks with the ceiling. While you shop it changes
color and ambiance to represent passing time, gently shifting
between dawn and dusk. I have no idea how this effects
socio-retail-psychology, but it is incredibly pleasant. You
reach into your wallet for the credit card, humming an old
Wayne Newton tune, considering the purchase of a black
velvet painting of Liberace, while the sky turns a delicious
soft pink starry fluff cloud dawn. All is well. Go ahead...Buy.
Buy. Bye-Bye.

HERMISTON, OREGON: I'm explaining to our eight-year-old that "hail the size of golf balls" doesn't happen in this part of the country when, you guessed it, an unprecedented storm plops 4-inchers, smashing watermelon crops and car windshields.

RATHDRUM, IDAHO: I've just been explaining to our 19-year-old that "tornadoes" don't happen in this part of the country, when....... (Film at eleven.)

LAKE CHELAN, WASHINGTON: Perfect weather. I float mindlessly on calm blue waters. I contemplate a group of 3 clouds. Cleverly disguised as cumulus nimbus, I begin to suspect that Steven Speilberg has picked this remote area to film his next feature. The clouds drifted into fish shapes... easy for any self respecting cloud. Then, supposedly due to wind and jet stream variances, they formed sleek amber UFO shapes. Impressive, but still certainly explainable. Even the next shift to pink whale and orange elephant was within (barely) plausible limits. But then these "clouds" joined and created light streams like a $12.95 admission light show. What was left of scientific logic tried to accommodate to such cerebral adjustments as light refraction, water reflection, air temperature, and moisture level...you know, God. But then they turned green. Pre-tornado green, Kermit the Frog Green, St. Patty's day beer green, over ripe kiwi fruit green, and then subtly dissipated back to blue sky. I'm glad there were witnesses.

MANSON, WASHINGTON: Blankets on the grassy hill in front of our condo we snuggle to watch shooting stars in the inky summer sky. We saw more satellites than we did shooting stars.... and we saw a plethora of stars.

HOLLYWOOD, CALIFORNIA: After watching Close Encounters of the Third Kind (again) and the new

71

Apollo 13 and seeing the "other side" of the mission, I think NASA and the media have had their way with us long enough. All this hoo-haw about UFO'S? The sightings I've had over the Siuslaw River, Woahink Lake and the Oregon Coastline can't hold a candle to secret military missions and Hollywood special effects technology.

Oh well, I have my own theories about who's running the show. I just remain grateful that the admission price to such magical productions, be they real or surreal, is only a glance skyward.

Survival tips de jour

1. Learn to fly.
2. Buy a telescope for someone.
3. Visit Big Sky Country.
4. Sit on your porch and make up stories about clouds.
5. Put luminescent stars on your bedroom ceiling.
6. Sleep under the stars.
7. Read the story of "Chicken Little".
8. Find out if you think the Ozone Layer needs protecting.
9. Ask an elderly person to describe their favorite piece of sky.
10. Look up.

Chapter 18

Prayer

If one is to survive life one must pray. This has little to do with religion in my opinion. Prayer is the absolute acceptance of human vulnerability and the acknowledgment of our sheer powerlessness over whether we survive or not. Prayer is the ritual which offers up our awareness of our total fragility.

Without prayer there is no survival because prayer is at the polar opposite of power. Some people talk of "the power of prayer." That power exists only in the fragments of our comprehension that we do not hold the power over life or death, and the poetry of that rendering can be in the form of a silent smile or a wordy oratory.

I have never met a person who came face to face with Death who didn't know what a prayer was. No matter what it looked like or sounded like, it was always the same prayer.

Some Handy Dandy Definitions:

Pray: (Webster)
Entreat, implore, introducing a question, request, or

plea, supplication, to address God with adoration, confession, supplication or thanksgiving

Pray: (Dr. Vali)

The Essential Breath, poetry, pain, life, smiles, laughter, tears, hope, terror, gratitude, absolute vulnerability, solemn, silly, waiting, belief, questions, anger, rages, demands, silence, open, song, private, holy, sacred chit-chat, hanging-out-with-a-best-friend-kind-of-relationship with God as you know God.

Let me make it as easy as possible. I pray. A lot. And mostly I pray that I am not left to my own devices because I am basically an idiot. I pray that I can see the miracles that are directed my way instead of missing them because I am so consumed by my own self. I think prayer is nifty. Prayer has saved my life.

Prayer didn't save my marriage, or my daughter, or my Mother, or my Father, or my grade in that stupid class in college or my finances or my beloved kitty cat from suffering. Prayer didn't give me good hair or skinny thighs. Prayer didn't give me a way to not feel the pain of Jenny's death or my anger at foreign policy or AIDS or starving babies in Africa. Prayer hasn't offered me good lottery numbers or a belief that I have a special place with God. Prayer doesn't make me feel chosen or unique. Prayer doesn't give me much at all. Prayer isn't about putting a quarter into a cosmic vending machine for me. It's about acting as if I was in a relationship with the rest of the universe and being honest about what is going on with me.

I pray when I am furious. I pray when I am grateful. I pray my rages and pray my humors. I guess what prayer is for me is about sharing what I have. And all that I have is my humanity. I offer that up. I offer up my loved ones and my enemies. I offer up my terrors and my hopes. I see it as recycling. I offer up all that I have and then get back something in return which may have the same energy but comes in a different form.

Once, as a child, I prayed for a sign from God and nothing happened. I wanted a little blade of grass to move so I would believe. Nothing. Twenty years later, when I was praying for the health of my child, I was walking in a field and everything became still. I stopped in the silence and was astonished to see just one blade of wheat move. My prayer was answered in that moment. Tidy.

I remember asking God to save my marriage once. Didn't happen. But what I got back later was a strength to survive the truth of the situation so that when I met my true soul partner I would be ready to save the "real marriage". Now, often, I simply ask, "What is the truth of this situation?" Sometimes the answer comes pretty fast. I do pray hard when I am sick hoping a magic thing will happen and I will be rescued from my experience. Sometimes I am. Other times I simply visualize myself sitting on a little stool in the presence of God waiting. Sometimes I pray for God.

Many religions teach us to pray in many different ways. Good. I guess that makes me dangerous, but I think if everyone prayed, and everyone prayed for all those who were praying prayers then I suspect things would settle down on our little chaotic planet. But I'm not a religious scholar.

Life is tenuous, temporary, fragile. Life is big and delicious and free. We think we are so in control until something like a little virus or a great hurricane or cyclone comes and huffs and puffs and blows our house down. And we sit upon our rubble and realize that our bluff has been called and we are vulnerable. I call it the Scrooge Syndrome. The sudden crushing realization that we are temporary. And in that moment all we have to offer is our humanness. And what better way to offer our humanness than in the form of a prayer.

Prayer isn't complicated. It's just hanging out in the sacred space between breaths in and breaths out. Oh, we can add fancy things to that space if we choose, and we can say our prayers are better than others, but that is like saying our breaths are better than others. And there may be bad breath but there are no bad breaths. I suppose it is a dangerous politically incorrect thing to suggest people pray. Oh well. Those of us who are trying to survive know its value and the rest of you will if the spaces between your breaths get uneven.

Tips De Jour

1. Pray your prayers don't say them.
2. Sing or dance your prayers some starlit night.
3. Don't be afraid of the word prayer, it's just a word.
4. Respect other people who pray different prayers.
5. Pray with a pal.
6. Pray for people who pray.
7. Pray differently than you prayed yesterday.
8. Pray the same way you prayed yesterday.
9. Don't be mad at prayer just because you were hurt by religion.
10. Pray for me.

Chapter 19

Border Crossing

Even if you have a Magic Ring, you need a passport to get to Tahiti. If I'd had one three months ago I could have gone to Tahiti. Bummer. If I'd had one last weekend, I could have used it crossing the border to Canada. It would have been helpful when the customs person scared us. Ever since living in the Republic of China and directly experiencing terrorism, I respect (and fear) being off USA soil without a passport. I got my new passport yesterday.

Some handy-dandy Definitions:

Passport: (Dr. Vali)
　　An identification document with a lousy photo
　　which is very, very cool to use at the grocery store
　　when cashing a check
Border: (Cartoons)
　　A dotted line on the earth

Border: (Dr. Vali)
An artificial line between here and there which tends to make people think they are different from one another
International Travel: (Dr. Vali)
Not an activity for the timid

Okay, I admit I am a bit of a paranoid. But after living overseas for a while I learned that my "American Arrogance" is handy for living in America and not that useful in other cultures. Not all countries appreciate cowboys. I have seen terrorism first hand. I was actually wounded in action directed at me because I was an American and for this reason I get a little case of heebie-jeebies when I cross borders. For example, when I was in Mexico recently I couldn't help but notice some random military activities. I pointed it out to my hubby but he didn't see it with the same eyes I did. It didn't keep me from shopping, of course, but I immediately made note of the American embassy address.

I sympathize with cultures who have been invaded and controlled. It reminds me of my first marriage. I have empathy because I lived in an Oregon Tourist Mecca for many years. Sacred ground is often ignored by strangers. Rules, rituals, rights and laws change from boundary to boundary, border to border. When people walk through your living room you expect them to remove their boots and not spit on the carpets. Be it ever so humble....take care of what's sacred.

I recently moved to a foreign culture (Washington State), learned a new language (I now speak a bit of Mitchell and beginning Step-parent), found sacred ground (the remote control), learned new customs (our mutual healing journey) and created new sanctuaries (our new deck). Precious and tender journey, marriage. Need a decent passport and respect for each other's boundaries.

So we're treating our blended family to a ferry expedition to British Columbia and get stopped at the border. The customs official looks in the back seat with "are-you-kidnapping-these-children-eye-contact" (a special training course for border officials). She interrogated our kids. They were amused until asked if they had seen their "other parent" lately. Our 8-year-old was worried and told the officer that she hadn't seen her birth mommy in a long time. (Border Crossing Nightmare number 87.) An intense professional investigation ensued. We (the alleged parents) were asked for more "Official Identification" and family photos. The wallet sized wedding photo of us in our perfect "match-the-color-swatch-from-Florence's-Bon-Jour" really threw them. Obviously we had planned this kidnapping thoroughly. As a red blooded American patriot I was ready to show my stretch marks from childbirth. Finally, the customs person discovered a long time to an 8-year-old was two days. I hope they do as thorough a job when someone is taking young boys across the border.

So, I got my new passport yesterday. Let's go someplace. But don't mind me if I look over my shoulder a bit. After all, I'm stuck with the same charming passport photo for 10 years, and just because it looks like it should have numbers under it doesn't mean anything. And in a world of twitchy global peace efforts, when everyone is out to get you, paranoia is just good thinking.

Survival tips de jour

1. Don't cut your hair just before a passport photo.
2. Carry all of your photo albums, slides, home videos scrapbooks and children with you everywhere.
3. Pay attention to who crosses your borders.
4. Don't ever let politics effect your shopping.
5. Don't ever let shopping effect your politics.
6. To honor someone else's sacred ground doesn't mean you engage in it or take it on as your own, you simple honor it as sacred to them.
7. Walk gently on Sacred Ground.
8. Everyone's Home is Sacred Ground.
9. If planet Earth is your home, then all of it is sacred ground.
10. Do not kidnap children, even your own.
11. Get a passport just in case you get an opportunity to travel to Tahiti next week.

Chapter 20

Angels

How could I write a compilation of my ideas, even my less than sterling ones, without referring to angels and their necessity in our survival? I couldn't.

Handy Dandy Definitions

Angels: (Webster)
   A spiritual being superior to man in power and intelligence, an attendant or spirit guardian, messenger

Angels: (Dr. Vali)
   Surprising teachers and reminders that there is an order to the universe

Maggie Mae: (Dr. Vali)
   My other cat

After my daughter Kirsha died she showed up in the dreams of several people who had never met her. She would arrive with a ball of light in her hands and proceeded to offer this light to their hearts. Angel work, me thinks. Angels are a hot ticket recently, but I think they have just gotten better press lately, because they have been here since recorded history. All the holy books of all major religions describe miraculous events via angel work. Some people find it difficult to believe in UFO's but find it easy to believe in angels. Other people find it difficult to believe in angels but easy to believe in UFO's. What are you gonna do? I myself have had several amazing encounters which I will probably detail another time over coffee if you are buying. I can say that one early angel encounter was very personal and very sweet. But that was before I knew that angels come in two disguises. Most people think angels come as beautiful and sweet mercies. I agree. However, I also know angels come in some very scary and disturbing forms under assumed names. The messages of miracles are not always wrapped in pretty paper, sometimes they are wrapped in the harsh, vile darkness of pain and horror. The lessons from those angels allow us to become the very miracle we want to believe in.

An Open Letter to my Angels: You Know Who You Are

If you are reading this letter then you are probably one of my **angels** and I want to send you a blessing. For many (many) years my life was filled with turmoil and grief, trouble and drama, chaos and crisis... Ah, the good old days!!! Many angels helped me survive to reach my dream. You know who you are. I had a dream that if I kept faith in my higher good, tried to use as much integrity as I could muster from moment to moment, if I could see my failures as lessons in the effort, and kept on keeping on, that somehow, someday it would matter and I would find peace, joy, love and serenity. I didn't have much to go on except a mustard seed of faith, a large dose of persistence... And a lot of angels. Angels who gave me blessings of light, money, hugs, a place to stay, a smile, a gift, a prayer, a phone call, an answer, a listening ear, a word of encouragement, an idea, a pat on the back, a kick in the behind, a challenging obstacle, another disappointment to overcome, a job, a touch on the cheek, a fantasy, a prediction, chocolate, a moment's peace, a book, a candle, an intimate moment with no strings, a view, a meal, a tragedy, a walk, a seashell, a loss, a letter, a poem, a tear, a laugh, a song, a rejection, a time with my kids, a memento, a respite, a terror to survive, another heartbreaking loss to rise above, a magical insight, a night of care during a deep dark night of the soul, a bowl of soup, a Diet Pepsi®, a tease, a joke, a coffee, a breath (or a breath mint) at just the right moment..... **I couldn't be here without you.** Through the years God generously supplied me with angels who guarded me, challenged me, tested me, broke my heart, healed my heart, wounded my spirit, opened my heart, and loved me enough to give me just exactly what I needed (whether I wanted it or not) to make it this far!

If through the years I didn't make it clear that I was grateful, please accept my gratitude today, now. If through the years I stepped on your toes please accept my apology now. If through the years I wounded you, please accept my apology now. If through the years I seemed desperate to survive and I didn't honor you, please accept my apology now. If through the years I didn't give as much as you gave, please accept my apology now.

83

And if through the years you were indeed horrible and awful to me, hurt me, wounded me, broke my heart and tried to break my spirit for your own selfish survival purposes, I now call you a blessing angel because I can now see ALL parts as a blessing. ALL IS BLESSING.

Miracles are increments of faith put in one context of time. My life is a miracle, and every detail has been the warp and woof of the fabric creating this weaving. So whether you are one of my strong beautiful angel strands or one of my angel twisted knots, I thank you. My tapestry is a magic carpet.

Thank you for your unique presence in my life. I hope your angels are giving you huge miracles.

Angel Tips De Jour

1. See the angels all around you.
2. Be someone's angel of mercy.
3. Thank your angels and discover the messages they have given.
4. Count the angels on the head of a pin.
5. Write anonymous angel notes to your angels.
6. Believe.
7. Do not fear angels in ugly disguises.
8. Be an angel magnet.
9. Create an angel bulletin board.
10. Ask your angels for assistance, they are waiting to serve you.

Chapter 21

Getting Into Hot Water

There is something important to be said for the intimacy of sharing in a cup of hot brew with a companion. A mug of coffee, tea, cocoa, spiced cider, or just hot water, can offer a warmth that seeps from the edge of a hand held mug to the conversation across the table. But more important than what you drink out of your mug, is whether there is a safe place you can go to find peace in a troubled world. And if that is a place where you can get a cup o' warmth, then you are well on your way to survival.

Some handy-dandy Definitions:

Water: (Dr. Vali)
What don't you understand about water?
Coffee: (Webster)
A drink made by percolation, infusion, or decoction from the roasted and ground or pounded seeds of

several trees or shrubs of the madder family/genus coffea seed.
Coffee: (Dr. Vali)
A tall Americano, with room

In the early 1970's I lived in the Republic of China and learned a few things about tea. Now I live in the 90's and know a few things about coffee. However, the tradition I have maintained over the years is to drink just hot water. In China the elders would drink a cup of near boiling water at bedtime as a sedative. Surprisingly enough it does not act as a diuretic and indeed it is a calming, centering and sensual pleasure. I have come to the habit of taking a cup of quite hot water after dinner...much to the bemusement of companions and waitresses alike. It seems a bit like a hot tub for the tummy and rumor has it that it helps metabolize protein more efficiently. I can't swear to that, but I like the notion.

For some odd reason I am terrified of prepackaged spiffy teas. You know the kind, with cute little pictures of animals in pajamas and fairy princesses sitting in trees kind of teas? I don't feel safe when I drink brew made out of some randomly picked unknown flowering plant. I have attempted to relieve my phobias of Conspiracy plots by the Tea Board, import tea warfare, visions of people picking tea leaves and mixing them with herbs and anything they could pick to fill up their quota, the entire political reality of the 60's, the Nixon years, Kent State, the hidden meanings behind Rocky and Bullwinkle, federal regulations and standards about tea-bag-paper, and so on. But like any other phobia there is no easy explanation. And what about The Boston Tea Party? It's a time honored tradition to fuss over tea. Oriental Tea Ceremonies or the MIF (Milk In First) controversy in England can be royal fussing. I once enjoyed a fuss in British Columbia over High Tea. Did you ever put tea bags on swollen eyes in the morning?

Tea is an ancient drink and a drink of the future. But reading the future must be difficult if the tea leaves are stuck in a bag. A friend reminded me that the Buddha drank green tea to stop war. I liked that. I'll try tea again.

But coffee is another topic. It took me a long time to appreciate coffee. My mom thought it the obligation of a young woman to drink coffee in preparation for her role in society. Fooey... Mom was an addict and tried to get me hooked. It didn't work.... Until... Well, it didn't work until I went to Disneyland and drank my first coffee filled with chocolate and whipped cream. Instant junkie material. Then my daughter worked at a major coffee chain and gave me free samples. And that was the beginning of a relationship with coffee.

But what I have learned most of all about these various brews is that the location and company are more important than what I drink. I meet old friends for a cup of java and new friends for a cup of orange juice. When I was an orphan trying to survive, I met my bestest pal who was a barista in a coffee shop. Once, when I had apparently paid enough dues as a local, she and her colleagues announced that I was no longer "counter scum," I was family. I sat by the counter on an old yellow kitchen stool and discussed the variences of the Universe from day to day and was no longer an orphan. It saved my life. If you can't drink coffee and won't drink tea, drink hot water and ask a friend out to talk over the state of the world or the weather. A lot of time when we are in Survival Mode we tend to isolate to nurse our wounds. And sometimes people try to nurse those wounds over a brew that is more addicting than coffee. Don't hide in your house, go O.T.D. and hang with a cup. After a while you will begin to recognize your new family. The ritual of "going out for coffee" isn't just for addicts and trendy Yuppies. This ritual is for any survivor who wants to perfect the hang.

Survival Tips de-jour

1. Use the phrase "spot of tea" to sound like you have been out of town.
2. Espresso yourself.
3. Tip heavily (many coffee engineers work long hours for low pay)
4. The Mad Hatter's tea-time was six o'clock. Four o'clock is considered by most as civil.
5. Go to the most expensive restaurant in town and for around a dollar or two you can have a cup of coffee and feel like you've been out on the town.
6. Remind yourself that Sophia Loren drinks a cup of espresso each morning as her first "beauty ritual."
7. Too much of anything can be dangerous.
8. Support coffee growing nations in other ways.
9. Don't spill the beans or get in Hot Water.
10. Let more than coffee percolate in your brain.
11. To participate in tea ritual is to celebrate the elegance of control.
12. Hum "Two for tea and tea for two, you for me and me for you..." while serving tea.

Chapter 22

Drive-by Questioning

I did a "drive-by" yesterday. I drove downtown. Behind the drive-through bank was a glorious bush of spring lilacs. I steered the jeep to the hedge edge, opened the window and grabbed some. No one saw me. Then I did a drive-by ATM for cash to buy a drive-by double tall mocha to drive back to my office. What's happening?

Some handy-dandy Definitions:

Questions: (Webster)
An interrogative expression often used to test knowledge in dispute or open for discussion
Questions: (Dr. Vali)
Driving forces which make me want to ask people for their thoughts and offer my own ideas and inquiries much to the annoyance of friends and

family but in fact why I became Dr. Vali because I had a few thousand kajillion questions I wanted answered and no one wanted to play

Drive-By: (Dr. Vali)
To quickly zoom past something in a vehicle and give it less attention than it deserves

I remember my parents horror as they read about the first drive-through churches in California. The concept of fast food religion drove them crazy. Of course, in those days it was acceptable if they did a drive-through to the man with the Texaco Star for total automotive service. They loved that. I got spoiled by living in Oregon. In Oregon you are not allowed to pump your own gas. In Washington I have to get out of my car to pump my own gas. Many moons ago I felt very hip and empowered by my own petroleum management...now I just want to drive-through.

That reminds me... I almost drove through a redwood tree once. California again. Dozens of highway ads enticed me to "DRIVE THROUGH A TREE. AMAZING!" Since I was in a 35 foot RV and needed a VW to drive though, I did a drive-by. A Drive-by treeing, I guess. A dear friend threw a salmon to me from his car once when he had caught a number of sweet ones and wanted to share. He and I called that a drive-by fishing. Sometimes when I reflect on the drive-bys of life my reflections aren't all happy. I worry. I worry about drive-by shootings in scary neighborhoods where I once let my sweet babies jump rope on the front lawn. I think people should be required to get out of their cars if they are going to kill innocent children. Is it me or are people beginning to just stay home and do drive-bys on the Internet because they are too afraid or too comfortable to get out of the chair or their car? And even though we now spend more time driving I think we may be losing our drive.

Some low impact former friends used to say I was "driven" because I wanted a PhD. I guess after all of my self-righteous denials they were correct. I was driven to change my poverty. I was driven to escape from violence. I was driven to rise above the common expectations of myself. These friends didn't inspire me and so they actually became drive-by friends with drive-by hit and run comments.

What turned on my drive were the inspirational events from two women in their late 70's and two younger women in their 30's. The older women were still working at "minimalist waged" jobs. They suggested that at 70 years plus I would still be female, probably be alone and still working. They drove home an appealing concept: *work less hours for more money.* The younger women were both victims of drive-by marriages. They had worked minimalist jobs to put husbands into "important careers" only to be left alone with a welfare check and the babies or the image of their now important husbands doing a drive-by child visitation with their new drive-by lovers. Those women drove home a point about life. Life takes some drive.

Life is a heartrendering drive-through and can drive some to drink. But please don't drink and drive. Perhaps this is why some people give up their drive for a better life while others open drive-through coffee kiosks to serve drive-by people who are driven to buy cellular phones to call their kids during their morning commute since they weren't there in the morning and won't be there at night. That just drives me crazy.

91

I guess my main question today is "what's the rush?" But sometimes survival is more about drive to survive than quality of the survival. Is it wrong to cut a hole in a tree so a car can go through it? Is it wrong to have a drive-by clinic? Of course not... Unless it leads to isolation and ignorance. I know I don't want drive-by neurosurgery, but then again drive-by donuts is just not a problem.

Survival tips de jour

1. Pick lilacs whenever you can.
2. Drive through trees ONLY when they are part of a tourism drive.
3. Don't drink and drive.
4. Drive is not a bad thing, it got many Americans across the Mississippi.
5. Participate in a Newspaper Drive for Charity in your community.
6. Don't forget the Red Cross Blood Drive.
7. If you are not able to drive your point home in a conversation, maybe you're point is pointless.
8. If you lose your drive, remember what the original mission was.
9. Don't let crazy people drive you insane, stay out of their way.
10. Take a Sunday drive...on Tuesday.

Chapter 23

Celebrations

Having just buried my daughter and then my Mother three weeks later....I admit that Halloween was hollow, Veteran's day reminded me of wars, Thanksgiving dinner was Chinese Food, Hanukkah candles dripped wax on my favorite table cloth, and the Christmas tinsel is dragging. Merry Whatever! To card carrying Holiday Addicts and those who put the Bah in Humbug....I salute your celebrant nature. Wait! I almost forgot...I am the Czarina of Holidays!! Celebrating is essential to survival.

Some handy-dandy Definitions:

Celebration: (Webster)
   To do something to show that a day or event is important
   To honor with festivities
   To make merry on such an occasion.

Celebration: (Dr. Vali)
See above and add food
Bah-Humbug: (Dr. Vali)
A fun thing to say when feeling cranky
Czarina: (Webster)
Feminine: a person with great authority
Czarina: (Dr. Vali)
See Diva
Diva: (Dr. Vali)
My new cat because Bill and Maggie Mae are dead (see Angels)

I have always adored the phrase "to make merry." It puts me into a Dickens of a mood and I find myself wanting to use the word "Fezziwig" in a sentence. As our cute little world becomes more chaotic in its move toward lasting peace...there often seems no apparent reason to celebrate. Losses, deep and abiding, are so annoying. And catastrophes are so incredibly pesky. A precious friend of mine suggests that compost creates perfect growing medium for Roses...but it smells awful. Thus, as we are surrounded by stinking thinking, decaying ideas, rotting philosophies, putrid notions, and rancid politics...it is the **Rose** that is the celebration. **Rose** petals dropped on church floors by flower girls or a **Rose** behind the ear of your lover. Dance with a **Rose** in your teeth to the Yellow **Rose** of Texas, or send a fan letter to someone named **Rose**. Lights of a Menorah celebrate the faithful who **Rose** to hope through darkness. Use **Rose**water, or Parsley, Sage, **Rose**mary and thyme, and look at the holidays through **Rose** colored glasses since one point of

Christmas is that eventually Jesus **Rose** and Easter means it's almost Spring!

Let's celebrate! Celebrations are essential to survival. Bring back old traditions or make new ones. Celebrate your survival each day, unless you want the only celebration associated with you to be your wake. Long weary winters can be quite damp and dreary without celebrations. If nothing else works, celebrate getting up this morning to another chance to choose cheery over cranky, compassion over cynicism, love over fear, and joy over grief. It is no coincidence that celebrations are associated with candles, lights and sparkling things...Lighten up your darkness or the darkness of someone else! Take a cake to an elderly person or a tablecloth and centerpiece to a fast food restaurant. Dance in an elevator and put a birthday candle in a sandwich. Anyone who has nothing to celebrate can celebrate the fact that they have nothing at all to celebrate. But they can now celebrate that event as the anniversary of the celebration called "We Have Nothing To Celebrate Day." There is absolutely no good reason not to celebrate. Even the darkest day of your universe can merely be defined as a day you eventually celebrate surviving. Buy confetti.

Survival tips de jour

1. Wear tinsel on your head, often.
2. Give candles or roses as presents.
3. Light a candle for someone.
4. Celebrate in your own way and celebrate the fact that someone else celebrates in their own way which may be different than your way of celebrating a celebration (Reread this if necessary).
5. Celebrate for no apparent reason, saying random HO, HO, HO's to complete strangers.
6. Give gifts anonymously.
7. Celebrate the opening of a new restaurant .
8. Keep seasonal lights on windows all year (except for the blinking ones because they are just too completely annoying).
9. Help an elderly or disabled neighbor put up holiday lights.
10. Get Lighter.

Chapter 24

Stendhal Syndrome

In 1817, the French novelist Stendhal collapsed when viewing the Niccolini Chapel in Italy. It could be that he didn't eat regularly, but he said this was caused by "the physical effects of being overcome by one's surroundings." I myself have collapsed from the effects of being overcome by the vision of my family room after a video marathon weekend. And I eat regularly. Very regularly. Since 1817, Stendhal Syndrome is the name given to an emotional response to great art. Since 1990, "Mom's having a tantrum" is the name given to my emotional response to the family room.

Some handy-dandy Definitions:

Fine Art: (Dr. Vali)
> Yeah, right! As though I would even try to be so presumptuous that I could define art... Ha, you must think I am a real idiot to go there, forget it.

Fine Art: (Someone)
I dunno what art is but I know what I like
Syndrome: (Webster)
A group of signs and symptoms that occur together and characterize a particular abnormality

Fine art is necessary for survival because without it there would be no point in being on the planet. I think fine art can be described as a brief and sacred capturing of the energy of the universe and can be distinguished from other stuff by the mere fact that it blows off your socks even when you aren't wearing any. Fine art isn't about who decides what is economically valued but rather by if and how it changes your experience on this planet. I have seen fine art created by children and by old crazy people. I have seen galleries full of non art and found a piece of art at a thrift store. The group agreement suggests that there are certain people who get to decide what is art and what is not. Not true. The test of great art is only time. And since most of us do not live for the centuries necessary to make the judgement we must boldly decide what we adore here and now. Many times I agree with the "knowers" of art. Many times I do not. So sue me. My eyes as well as your eyes contain the capacity to recognize God in a variety of forms. Not just people with lofty positions on art critique boards. In fact, few people recognized the Baby Jesus as a Messiah. But that tricky God put it in an interesting art form. A baby. Art also must be viewed with the eyes of some sort of faith in the Universe. And some people CAN see better than others because their eyes are wide, wide open. A guy named Stendhal saw too well I guess. In fact, that is why they named the syndrome after him.

The Stendhal syndrome "touches people who make themselves vulnerable to the stimulation that is unique to unique destinations." (I'm not sure if the definition includes places like Casa de Fruta or Graceland.) Many individuals report collapsing at the Holocaust Museum, the Kennedy Memorial, and other great historical sites. Another interesting malady, the Jerusalem Syndrome, is "specific location dependent" but linked to people with previous psychiatric history. Some individuals go to Jerusalem burdened with delusions that they are determined to fulfill in the Holy land. Some, for example, are compelled to act out John the Baptist behavior. Or the crucifixion drama. But Stendhal Syndrome is more akin to the overwhelming passion associated with experiencing Michelangelo's David or the Sistine Chapel.

Stendhal Syndrome can also be experienced by hearing tremendous works of music. Many weep hearing La Boheme or Handel's Messiah. It is true that some individuals weep hearing the entire guitar solo of Stairway to Heaven. But that is another syndrome for another discussion.

San Francisco. Random gallery. Bronze lifesize sculpture of a human form in a yoga position. Dr. Vali goes bye-bye. I hyperventilate, knees become weak. Dizzy. I walk around the piece. Could I sell everything I own to get $50,000? I had to sit down. It only lasted a few moments but changed how I view art forever. Something shifted. I grokked the difference between art and ART. ART is alive and in its presence you are changed.

Arizona. Random Southwest Art Gallery. Usual array of pots, weavings, baskets. On a shelf sits an

99

indistinguishable sculpture. From a distance it looks like a lump of black adobe with flecks of color. It calls. It demands attention. I get closer. Eyes begin to water, blood pressure elevates. It is 118 degrees outside...yet I shiver. This profound impressionistic representation of a traditional Hopi home captured the truth of presence. It called to soul. I saw the history of the people, smelled the campfires and heard the songs. Children ran free and women smiled. Sunbrowned skin wrinkled on the foreheads of elders. My nervous system put my body on auto pilot as I was exposed to a powerful work of art.

Washington D.C. The Wall. Veterans and family, senior citizens, loud kids with skateboards, nondescript tourists, me. Our pilgrimage through the art form bonds us in silence and reverence. Names of soldiers leap off the black marble. Their voices are a roll call. All names become someone I know personally. I grieve each individually and collectively. My heart rate increases. Tears. Breath. Weakness. Movement, flow, shape, size, energy. This art is living presence and I was permitted to enter its soul for a few holy, transforming, healing moments. Honored. Faint.

They would have had to haul poor Mr. Stendhal out on a stretcher.

Choosing to be vulnerable to grand art or history causes this curious syndrome. I hope they don't find a cure. ART appreciation is definitely an important survival strategy and not a job for wimps!

Survival tips de jour

1. Spend money on art.
2. Try to see big art.
3. Support the arts.
4. Be vulnerable to your soul stirrings in the presence of art.
5. Travel to see art.
6. Wear art.
7. Touch art.
8. Listen to art.
9. See art.
10. Be art.

Chapter 25

Why Say More?

Please pardon my brevity and redundancy, but some life moments offer no other choice. It's like sunsets. Sure, one happens every day, but some sunsets are incredible and far beyond verbal description. So, you resort to brevity and redundancy and mutter an intelligent, "Wow!"

Some handy dandy definitions

Wow: (Dr. Vali)
What don't you understand about Wow?

Yesterday I found myself completely exhausted from the basic efforts involved in staying alive....you know, general day to day human struggles. Although my soul was light, my day to day burdens had been quite inundating. In fact, I was too pooped to create a respectable pop. It was 9:20 P.M. and I was still at my office. I looked at my remaining paperwork and whined. There was no one there to hear it. I was very annoyed with the demands of my day job, since it was seriously cutting into my art and recreation time.

(Translation: The drama czarina was having a long and annoying Monday, it was late, no dinner, I saw no end to the darkness of human existence, I had writer's block, "bleak" looked like hope from where I stood, and my imagination...the heart of my art....was "closed until further notice".)

I turned on the radio. To my grateful soul's resuscitation came the first notes of Aaron Copeland's *Fanfare for the Common Man*. That amazing piece of art was immediately followed by John Williams' *Olympic Fanfare, 1984*. My tired and cranky heart cracked open and I wept. I called the radio station to confirm the title, and as I shared a memory of my daughter actually playing this music in a symphony at age 13, the D. J. wept with me. Our voices broke as we shared our heart's euphoria and we both tumbled head over heels into the balm of the music.

Once again I was gently reminded, in complete absolute terms, down to the toes of my soul, that all the Universe is in divine order.....even when it looks like a mess. Life must be perfect and completely correct if such a music can exist. All worldly matters pale in the presence of the Divine, which is gloriously revealed in Fine Art. I have nothing more to say. It's hard to get me speechless, but some things are bigger than words. **Wow!**

Survival tips de jour

1. Don't try to perfect perfection.
2. Turn off the TV and turn on the radio once in a while.
3. Go to children's band concerts, even if you don't have a kid.
4. Believe.
5. Create a Fanfare.
6. Be a Fanfare.
7. Write your own music.
8. Seek Harmony.
9. Ask yourself, if you were a sitcom, what would your theme song be?
10. Find things to say Wow about.

Chapter 26

A Bowl of Heartsoup

The phone rang. At the other end was one of my brilliant friends. After initial "Hi, howaryas", we eagerly began one of our typical conversations. You know, chit-chat.

Some handy-dandy Definitions:

Chit-Chat: (Webster)
    Small talk, gossip
Chit-Chat: (Dr. Vali)
    Includes but isn't limited to:
    • the reorganization of the Known Universe
    • defining our interior life "homework"
    • asking "what is the Truth of all things?"
    • laughing at how the universe seems to laugh at us
    • sharing gratitude about obstacles which always become grand life lessons

- **exchanging joys about current victories and celebrations**
- **offering strength and hope to each other**
- **relishing an abiding belief that even small contributions matter in the big picture**

After our typical chit-chat settled into the mundane topics of conspiracy theories and our expected hopes about the long term patterns of global peace it occurred to us that we had never shared a recipe. We had never exchanged much of anything that would be considered by many as chit-chat normal. We had never once exchanged casserole secrets, sports scores, fishing or makeup tips. We didn't exchange hairdo wisdom or where the next fashion explosion might land hemlines. We didn't know each others favorite color or rock group and had never exchanged giggly insights into the men in our lives. In fact, such regular howsyourday-chatty-matter only added up to about .03% of our conversations. We wondered if we had lost track of such simple pleasures as mundane interaction in our quest for survival.

We agreed that our lives were more complicated then when Mrs. Cleaver (God love her) was everyone's neighbor. We knew we weren't alone because many of us have had to reinvent ourselves and we have had to ask new questions, and create new recipes for living. It's been hard on Betty Crocker (God love her) and hard to understand Martha Stewart (God love her). It honestly used to matter what kind of starch to use to help keep a spouse's shirt in shape. It really used to matter who had a good and economic casserole recipe to share which would feed 5 kids, a picky spouse and a live-in mother-in-law. During the Depression it really mattered how to best save a piece of string in case there might not be more available for 8 months. But the world has changed and so has survival.

While some of us have had to come home to tend the fires and raise the babies, others have had to go out to hunt the buffalo to keep homefires burning. (No wonder some of us are cranky.) The expectations of the current century have exceeded our capacity to trivialize life. Certainly there are the folks who still maintain this is the truth (God love them) but with the shrinking of the globe and all the stuff which goes with that (read your daily headlines) it hasn't seemed like a worthy survival task to refine chat-skills. However, it is a worthy survival skill to find a good recipe for soup. Always. Soup is ABSOLUTELY necessary to survive, no matter the century. In fact, I think a good bowl of soup may have the potential to save the earth and all its people. But that would have to be one amazing recipe. Now, I make a great soup or two and have a few secret recipes, but here is one that my pal and I decided might add to the survival repertoire. Pull out a bowl and grab a spoon.

Heartsoup
(Serves 2 or more)
Ingredients:
Huge portions of gratitude
Extract of pure humor
Add Faith (not fear)
A portion of curiosity
Multiple questions (equal portions of answerable and unanswerable)
Emotional Accountability

Ample tears for the Human Dilemma (avoid
   victimhood)
Ample hope for the Human Dilemma (avoid arrogance)
Large Pinch of Bravery
Dash of intentionality
One level head of Rational Thinking
Two portions of listening with every portion of
   speaking
Large measure of humility
Essence of silliness

Heartsoup tips de jour

1. Let pain dissolve quickly and ventilate as necessary.
2. Try on ideas for size.
3. Stir with generous portions of Belly Laughter, and cook
    in the heat of lively discussion.
4. Place in a context of prosperity and avoid any
    suggestion of lack.
5. Avoid attachment to outcome (results may vary
    depending on the agenda of the Divine).
6. Prepare to eat words if necessary.
7. Don't lie.
8. Apologize often (more frequently if necessary).
9. Forgive everyone for doing what it takes to survive
    (unless their survival style threatens your survival
    style).
10. Bless the process.

Serving Suggestion:
Serve from the heart, spilling generously all over
everyone.

Chapter 27

Fashion

I'm no slave to fashion but I didn't know what to wear today. The thought occured to me that it really didn't matter. Survival doesn't depend upon fashion of clothing as much as fashion of the heart and soul. What is my soul going to wear today? What sleeve should I put my heart on this afternoon? Will I skirt the issues or cloak my fears? Shall I throw my hat in the ring or remain a loafer? Am I clothed in Light or Darkness? Am I wearing armor or magnets? Am I covered in velcro or teflon?

Some handy-dandy Definitions:

Fashion: (Webster)
    A prevailing custom (as in dress)
Fashion: (Dr. Vali)
    A prevailing question (as in what to wear today)

I wrote a play about Men's Fashions once. It was a musical. When I saw it produced I realized it wasn't finished yet. I needed to complete the emotional wardrobe of the main characters. As life has seasoned me, I suspect I could rewrite the play now and it would be better. Fashion used to matter to me in the whole "dress for success" thing... Then I moved to the Oregon Coast where one dresses for survival and that is successful dressing. I went to New York for a meeting and the people there recognized me as from "Out West". It totally amused me because I didn't suspect that I would stand out. And I wasn't even wearing flannel at the time. Fitting in to the fashion scene can make you a member of an elite club. I've always been a member of my own club and so far that has helped me survive. I hope I become enormously rich and famous just so I can become an icon of fashion so I can laugh at it and help others to laugh also. I had a dream one night:

Fashion was an elegant woman who stepped out of her limo into the wind. Her perfect hair wrimpled in the breeze and her earrings schinckled little bell sounds as her tall slender body moved gracefully down the street. At first no one saw her because as she moved her form would rearrange to please whoever she met. She was a Shapeshifter.

Fashion spent her time snooping through everyone's closets so she could change her mind in a whim. She made her decisions in secret and made her public pronouncements in loud righteous tones. When she spoke, many strained to hear her disingenuous voice. When she spoke, the poor shuddered in shadows, and the colorblind winced. When she spoke the overweight sighed deeply and reached for chocolate while the anorexic weakly danced in the streets. When she spoke the too tall slumped and the too short

110

strained on tired toes to see what the fuss was about.

She always had to be the center of attention, and when she tossed her scarf over her shoulders, career women ran madly to department stores to buy scarves. She buttoned a top button and men in suits improved their posture and straightened their ties. Some risked getting close to see if she was wearing makeup today and others genuflected in rites of shoe worship and accessory glory. She ignored them all. She was on a mission.

She was looking for her lover again, and still could not find him. He had deserted her for a round shaped woman in hand-me-downs who didn't worry about Fashion. He loved her honesty, her laughter and her heart. She loved him for his mind and thought that his soul was precious.

When he dressed up for work she would hug him and say his ties were cute. "Ties aren't cute," he'd scoff in feign annoyance, "they are essential to the perception of power and corporate climbing." And she would just laugh again. He adored her and he was hooked. It wasn't his fault. All of Fashion's hard work was manipulation and narcissistic and tedious and didn't soothe or delight his soul. His round shaped woman wore whatever she wanted and was always ready to laugh in the presence of honesty and pretense. Sometimes he would scold her about laughing at his ties or suits so that he could hear her sing him a little song:

Beauty is an inside job, a magic gift of soul
Fashion's just the wrapping, it doesn't make the whole.
Grab some sparkley fabric or newsprint and a string
Beauty ain't the feathers, dear, it's how the birdies sing.

Survival tips de jour

1. Sit in a hotel and watch the people go by and pretend it is a sociological study of fashion.
2. Create a hand-me-down network.
3. Make a memory quilt out of your old clothing.
4. Frame a T-Shirt from a foreign country.
5. Help someone else dress for success.
6. Don't judge a book by its cover.
7. Give the clothes you hate which stay in your closet for years and years and years to someone who has no money for clothes.
8. Start a hat collection.
9. Wear 2 different colored socks.
10. Try something different.

Chapter 28

Socks

I'm sort of down in the dumps today. It's 4:15 PM and it's dark. I hate daylight savings time. Winter. The season of **Hallowthankmas** is upon us and nostalgia and grieving mix into my wassail cup like a bitter brew. Sparkling lights and fattened poultry dishes are grim reminders of materialism and the imbalances of a world gone mad. How can we eat until we burst when countless beings on our planet are dying for a spoonful? Peacemakers are murdered and lunatics run free to add multidimensionally to their golf scores and credit card bills. It's starting to bug me. If it weren't for socks I might just join the other side and say to hell with survival of the soul.

Some handy-dandy Definitions:

Socks: (Contemporary lingo)
    The name of a somewhat famous cat
Sox: (Sports types)
    A Baseball team

Socks: (Kids)
Punches in the arm
Socks: (Dr. Vali)
Big smuggly-wuggly cozy things which go on your feet and make life all better again

When life just gets too overwhelming, I go to my sock drawer and pull out a pair of smoodgie foot huggers and suddenly the world is softer. Warmer. Quieter. All the rough edges are a bit smoothed out, and padding around the planet becomes an act of intimacy rather than contact conflict. Slippers or bare feet, although honest in their own realm, do not offer the condolences and compassions of a properly socked foot. Metaphor suggests the foot is symbolic of our "under-standing" in the world. When my understanding is protected by thick cotton, wool or a lovely blend of fabrics and colors, somehow my consciousness begins to open to gentle thoughts and tender missions. Indeed, many religions and cultures demand the removal of footwear in sacred places, while some societies require this simple etiquette only at threshold of home. I like that.

Here's what I think. If every World Leader had to enter a meeting, mediation or negotiation in sock feet, I think things would go better. I suspect some of you may immediately become concerned about global sock-odor, but just as baking soda can neutralize those less than charming fragrances, socks somehow neutralize stinky attitudes. Heads of state in socks might speak more softly or in quieter tones. They might use more compassionate language. Instead of budget cuts and tax freezes some might suggest warm woollies or cotton blankets for the poor or elderly during freezing weather.

In applying this to real life (whatever that means) even if your rules say you can't wear socks to anything but a sockhop, you can come home after your big-deal-grown-up life and put socks on immediately. I recently spent a week in Seattle receiving advanced training in Mediation with other professionals who know that things have to change for PEACE to happen. One favorite moment of this intense educational event was an impromptu break that led to a gathering of folks over a cup of coffee. We shared a fascinating, cutting edge, whimsical, challenging, bright, fun, energetic, state of the art, globally dynamic discussion with several brilliant world class professionals......in our sock feet. Big ideas. Powerful words. Soft edges. Hallelujah.

When you are in your socks it's more difficult to trample people and it is easier to survive the harshness of reality which often shows up in big black boots. Sock it to me!

Survival tips de jour

1. Wear fun socks inside your logger boots.
2. Give socks for gifts.
3. Instead of a coffee break, take a sock break.
4. Make sock puppets.
5. Save money in a sock and sock it away for a rainy day.
6. Buy a new pair of socks and never wear them, simply keep them handy in case you need them. You will never feel poor if you have a new unopened pair of socks ready.

7. Do what my daughter does when she needs to make a statement, wear unmatched socks and don't apologize for being creative and fun.
8. Recycle old socks as dust clothes or dog toys.
9. Donate socks to charity.
10. Wear bright colored socks to bed if you are sad.

Chapter 29

See You in 5 Minutes...

My youngest daughter and I have a good-bye tradition which anyone can use. Like many ancient rituals, ours is based on a special history. She was born with a rare pancreas disorder. Her condition led to 13 years of grueling diagnostic examinations, invasions, x-rays, surgeries and failed interventions. There was apparently no treatment, no clear diagnosis, no intervention, no cure, no hope of her having a pain free existence. Every time she was wheeled away for another series of tests, exams or surgeries, I would weep, pace, worry, pray, twitch and eat my way through the terrifying wait never knowing if she would survive. Rituals become survival skills. Rediscover your old rituals or make up new ones.

Some handy-dandy Definitions:

Rituals: (Webster)
    A ceremonial act
Rituals: (Dr. Vali)
    Lifevests in a scary world

117

In the ongoing years of hospitalization, I had seen too many babies die. It just changes how you see life. So each time Kyrin was taken down a hall it would feel like a hundred years until she returned. But when she woke up in the recovery room, she thought it had only been a few minutes that had passed, not lifetimes. On one such adventure through medical intervention, we began our ritual. We would say good-bye with a hug and smile. We would look deeply into each other's eyes and say an enthusiastic, "See you in 5 Minutes." After all, we decided, that's what good reunions feel like. When the waiting is over the pain of the waiting is gone.

We tested it in reverse when I went on a 10 day professional lecture trip away from home. And sure enough, my little girl said it felt like 5 minutes with our airport reunion hug. After that trip we decided that if one of us died, our spiritual reunion would erase the pain of waiting. The survivor would have a tough "5 minutes." But the reunion would be amazing.

The years passed quickly and my baby grew up. A surgical procedure invented when she was a teenager created a treatment which changed her painfilled life. She moved on as all children must. But, because of her experiences she is an ancient and wise soul in a beautiful young body. We kept our tradition in tack and used it for camp, band trips, business trips, and overnight slumber parties. Most parents are touched when they see their children go off to any activity, and when a child goes off to college it is such a victory of life. But when my beautiful, healthy, 6 foot tall, energetic and bouncy-filled-with-life daughter flounced off to her first freshman class it was a major mommy moment. Her bright and cheery, "See you in 5 Minutes, Mom" was much more than a regular teenage good-bye.

Only a few short months would pass before her big sister would die very unexpectedly of Insulin Dependent Diabetes. Three weeks later my Mom, the girls' grandma, died suddenly of heart failure. These were horrifying and precipitous and penetrating good-byes. What gets us through some of our most difficult moments is knowing we will be having a grand reunion in about "5 minutes."

There are cultures which give up their rituals and then the cultures die. Rituals give our lives meaning and can be the glue which holds us together when the wind blows. It doesn't have to be a religious event to be a ritual but it often becomes sacred if our hearts are involved.

Survival tips de jour

1. Don't ever leave in anger.
2. Write love notes to loved ones.
3. Life is short. Life is precious. Preserve it with your own unique rituals which become memories unless they become demands and prisons.
4. Study the rituals of another culture. Borrow one and honor it for an afternoon.
5. Take your children out for ice cream or show them the stars. Pick a day that is your annual Special Ice Cream and Stars Day.
6. Create reunions. Create new rituals. Reclaim old ones.
7. Don't procrastinate visiting that person you always say you are going to go see anyday now because 5 minutes comes and goes so quickly.
8. Don't miss rites of passage.
9. Let your children go and have their lives and make new rituals that match your relationship with your grown up children.
10. Make every 5 minutes count.

Chapter 30

Visible Statements

I have friends with tattoos. Visible statements projected on the epidermis. Bumper stickers. Communication. Personal calling cards, word pictures, mind statements, visual ramblings. Some call it art.

Others call it offensive. Jihad. One person's sacred is another person's secular. Holy War. Mecca or Medina. Them or Us. Where is the middle ground? Not Ground Zero, but DMZ. Checkpoint Charlie. Safe. Balance.

I wish my tattoos were only skin art. I don't have any of those. My tattoos are on my psyche.

Some handy-dandy Definitions:

Tattoo: (Webster)
> An indelible mark or figure fixed upon the body by insertion of pigment under the skin or production of scars

Psychic Tattoo: (Dr. Vali)
> Opinions. Beliefs. Prejudices. Values. Illusions. Scars. Fixed upon the human psyche by insertion of

others opinions, beliefs, prejudices. Stuck as permanently to one's being as an indelible mark of pigment on the epidermis. Psychic tattoos are also very hard to remove.

I was born female, Aries, White, America Northwestern, Christian, Hawkins, middle-class, birth ordered as baby, fourth generation showbiz culture....baby tattoos. Then I went into the world. There I was indelibly marked by my experiences. Emancipation. Violence. Washington. Marriage. China. Hippies. California. Vietnam. Childbirth. College. Oregon. Career. Other World Religions. Arizona. Divorce. New York. Art. Music. Education. Travel. Gay friends. Mexico. Medicine Women. Moving Vans. More wars. Sufi Dancers. Politics. Jewish friends. Earthquakes and Volcanos. Artists. People of Color. International Terrorism. Death. Native American friends. Poisonous snakes. Lovers. Hawaii. Afro-American friends. Books. Poverty. Rages. Films. New marriage. Children playing in open sewage in Third World Countries. Cancer. Alcoholics and Drug Addicts. Asian friends. Death. The Women's Movement. The Men's Movement. College. Musicians. Disneyland. Homelessness. Guam. Canada. Oceans. Deserts. Catastrophes. Miracles. This and that and that and this and that and the colors and borders and designs of my psychic tattoos began flowing into each other. It was as if other tattoos spilled all over my canvas. I began seeing the reflection of my tattoos and had to step back for proportion...and saw myself. Were my values art or madness? Were my perceptions Truth with a capital T?

I just have so much to learn. It's annoying. I think I know something, then I run into someone with a completely different frame of reference. I have to add or subtract from my inner tattoos to survive this life. Some examples:

•Altering your notions of the cow's position in life after living in Asia where rice farmers take their water buffalo into the house at night.

•Thinking you have knowledge about scuba diving until you fall overboard and actually meet the shark.

•Visiting the filthy houses of poor women and children as a well meaning human service worker and finding you must officially redefine "adequate" based on state legislation.

•Getting out of town or out of the country and finding that your little corner of paradise is indeed paradise and that most people feel that way about wherever they live.

•Seeing a young vital friend die too soon and having death in your living room instead of a million miles away .

•Finding that your best pal who goes to the PTA with you on Tuesdays has been mainlining cocaine for the last 11 months and realizing you didn't have a clue and still seeing her as a sweet wonderful soul and not some hooker in a gutter, she's still your friend and now your teacher.

•Finding out your spouse has betrayed you and everything you believe is wrong.

•Finding out what you think just isn't big enough, or strong enough, or good enough, or powerful enough, or clever enough to matter to everyone and, in fact, some people despise you.

•Expanding your mind beyond your own opinion while maintaining your own integrity.

We make local and global decisions based on our opinions, beliefs, prejudices, values. And sometimes we make decisions based on illusions. Some tattoos are pretty. Some

123

are not. My mom used to say, "pretty is as pretty does," actions speak louder than words. We may be able to cover up the ink type of tattoos, but we can't hide our psychic tattoos, they show up at the same time we do. Our psychic tattoos are a necessary part of survival because we need to have opinions and make decisions and discernments. On the other hand it really isn't necessary to force our tattoos on anyone else. I can't imaging someone forcing an ink tattoo on me or you. But isn't the world just filled with folks who would love to force their opinion on you? Scary.

Survival tips de jour

1. Think.
2. Don't be so sure you know all there is to know.
3. Question.
4. Celebrate your truth while staying open to other truths that also exist.
5. Reinvent yourself if you want to do so.
6. Temporary tattoos are a fun way to see if something fits.
7. Understand the difference between permanent and temporary.
8. Avoid forcing your tattoos on your children before they even know what their favorite color is.
9. Draw fun pictures on the bottom of your feet with a ball point pen.
10. Remember you have choices.

Chapter 31

Friends

George Baily discovered that friends were necessary for his survival. And, in the last scene of Frank Capra's 1946 movie, *It's a Wonderful Life*, he opens a book of Mark Twain to find this inscription from his angel:

Dear George,
Remember no man is a failure who has friends.
Thank you for the wings.
Love, Clarence

Some handy-dandy Definitions:

Friend: (Webster)
One attached to another with affection
Friend: (Dr. Vali)
Donna
Friend: (Dr. Vali)
Acquaintance, crony, well wisher, intimate, confidant, other self, comrade, mate, companion,

chum, pal, buddy, cohort, consort, side-kick,
playmate, compatriot, the fidus achates, FRIEND.
Friends: (From Ashley's third grade class) (Unedited)
trustwerethey
it takes two people
someone who lissins
help you when they are hert
cairing and funny
cheers you up
plays with you
play fair and don't cheet
not bossy
ushually agree and trueful
safe
helps you when your down in the dumps
helps with homework
never pushes you
never throw snowballs at you when you don't
    want them to
never cworel
help you up when you topple
kind
lets you do whatever you want
never gives up
invites you to a party or comes to yore
    brthday and give you a present
respects your body
won't steel your toys
won't brag or hit you
shares and doesn't yell at you
gives piggy back rides
dusent call you names

"Friendship, friendship...it's the perfect blendship" says the old song. No matter the word used, if you check your circle, clique, company, coterie, or personal society...there is probably at least one other being to whom you are attached by affection or esteem. If you have no friend on this cute little planet of ours, check to see if you have a pulse.

Our world seems to be getting a bit edgy about friendship. America, for example, used to be billed as a friendly nation. We would extend our hand across the global fence. Now, it seems that the same voices who once called for global well wishing are concerned about "friends" crashing through our borders and taking our jobs. Friends sit over espresso debating if sending troops and weapons to Genocidoville or supplying food to our starving neighbors in Nonplethoraopolis is a friend's duty. Whether global or next door neighbors, it is such a struggle to survive that rarely does a friendly cookie or recipe cross over the fence of the 90's. Some say technology is our friend and finding cyberfriends on the net may be the clique de jour. My computer is user friendly, I wonder if I am. Without computers, phones, faxes, e-mail, or our friends at the post office it is hard to keep in touch with friends. But real friends have a wonderful way of maintaining an ongoing conversation, no matter how much time has elapsed between sentences or physical proximity. New friendships must be tested by time, and time tests all friendships. I have friends I've never met, friends I've spent 20 minutes with and stayed in touch with for 23 years, friends of decades lost forever, reclaimed old ones, and dumped a few false friends. Make new friends but keep the old...reminds me of a little song about friendship I used to sing with my babies..."If I was a little bee, you would be the buzz. If I was a little peach you would be the fuzz. Good friends should stay together....."

What is the glue that holds a friendship together? Perhaps shared history, values, time and common mission is the adhesive. Survival, for example, makes deep friendships in foxholes. It's been said a zillion times, "to have a friend, be one". What does it take to be a friend? Look at your friends as if they were a mirror of yourself...and you will know!

A Handy Dandy Dr. Vali Haiku:

New friends compared lives
Discovering they were one,
Their dreams much the same.

A Handy-Dandy Bit of Dr. Vali Poetry

Friendship lives between dream and dreamer
And is the glue between idea and schemer.
Settled in between heart and lover,
Friendship can come with child and mother.
Found in the space between inhale and exhale,
It lives in necessity between Plankton and Whale.
Lodge Pole Pine is birth friend with fire,
And gluttony buddies are Chocolate and Desire.
Visions and Holy Ones are companions near,
While Desperate Depressions hold Victims dear.
I worked with a man just the other day,
Who didn't want his PAIN to go away.
PAIN had been his constant friend
While his other friendships had crashed to an end.
I suggested that he take his PAIN out to tea,
And thank it profoundly for its loyalty.
Then gently bow from deep in the soul
To claim a new vision of being whole.
PAIN was his lover who demanded his time
While never giving him much that was sublime.
So he bid his dear constant friend to depart
And promised to visit from distance, by heart.

Survival Tips de jour

1. Grab a friend and make your own list of famous friends.
2. Be a friend.
3. Befriend someone friendless.
4. It takes a long time to have an old friend. Have patience. Be a better friend.
5. Treat your spouse as well as you treat your best friend.
6. If your spouse is your best friend then you are lucky and should go out to ice cream and celebrate your grand fortune.
7. Look for friends in unexpected places with assumed names and false identities... Sometimes they start as enemies and end up as friends.
8. Invite your friends to meet each other.
9. Remember everyone can have friends. Even nasty people have friends. No one is immune to friendship.
10. Spend the afternoon talking to God as though He were your best friend. Take him out for Ice cream, your treat, of course.

Chapter 32

Cheap Thrills

I was thrilled to see the first crocus of the season. It was a survivor of another winter. So was I. I called friends to share my excitement. Cheap thrills. A critical survival element.

Some handy dandy definitions

Cheap: (Contemporary usage)
    A bargain, purchasable below the going price,
    gained with little effort
Thrills: (Webster)
    Something that causes an experience of excitement
Fame: (Dr. Vali)
    Fleeting Cheap Thrill

This month my travels have been less than exotic and more than remote. The common denominator has been cheap

131

thrills. I had a project in a small town in Washington....not an abyss, but definitely not the epicenter of culture or socio-ethnic diversity. During a break I drove my jeep further up the mountains to a little town called Roslyn. Roslyn was the fictional Cicily, Alaska in the TV series *Northern Exposure*. Being near fame is like being in a state of quasi-fame....a cheap thrill. You aren't really famous, with all the demands and requirements, but you are temporarily in the soup of it. I walked through sets enjoying recognizable elements from past shows. Then I drove around the town. I wanted a happy word to describe what I saw. I wanted it to be a word that wasn't judgmental but had difficulty finding one that said poverty gently? I was offered the word "minimalism". What a great word! Indeed, there was a minimum of new paint, new cars, and new construction. There was a minimum of new clothing stores, food sources, entertainment or art. It made that other little town I saw look sumptuous.

My next project took me to small town in Eastern Oregon. This town made Roslyn look like a boom town in comparison. But, it seems that no matter where I went that week I found a good cup of coffee in some local hang and listened to folks talking about local stuff, raising kids, or exchanging connections of hearts, minds, and souls. A significantly age-enhanced woman stopped and raved about my nifty green hat. It must have been her cheap thrill de jour. She didn't look like she got out much. Although a minimalist lifestyle certainly becomes a challenge to spirit and creativity, I have discovered, especially in the days when I was a single mom on welfare, that one has a choice to become bitter and cranky or become easily entertained. I suggest grabbing those rose colored glasses my darlings!

I used to teach a class called "Budget Romance" for economically challenged couples who were still in love. The participants had terminally ill children. My favorite story is about a couple who would go to a local greeting card shop. They couldn't afford to make a purchase so they would choose and exchange cards inside the store and return them to the racks. Cheap thrills! I am sure they went home to a warm evening.

Last weekend my family took a cheap thrills vacation. We grabbed the kids and drove **all the way** across town (away from the phone and pets) and "camped out" in a budget motel with a pool and jacuzzi and HBO and free continental breakfast. We spent three dollars on cheesy matching shirts and went bowling. We drove to the top of the highest local hill and played twenty questions in the car and watched the sunset. We went to the local Homeshow and got all the free samples we could and came back to our hotel and played cards in our room. It was a hoot. Cheap thrills.

Life is short. What really matters is soul connection and it doesn't take money to have a miracle. A friend was complaining that he believed he lost his lover because he didn't have money. I tried to tell him that he wasn't missing money, he was missing "wealth." He didn't get it. Ghandi is attributed with saying, "it takes no money to be clean and dignified" and Oscar Wilde with "life is too important to take seriously." Put these together and I see a life that is classy, elegant, beautiful, silly, graceful, light, inexpensive, holy and chipper. Although it certainly makes a trip to Maui easier it doesn't take a credit card to have a life of grace.

Survival tips de jour

1. Have popcorn parties during thunder storms.
2. Put handmade lovenotes in lunch boxes.
3. Toss flowery blooms from the garden into your bath.
4. Hunt and peck tunes on a piano from an old song book.
5. Host indoor picnics or outdoor poetry readings.
6. Make new rules for old card games.
7. Visit a local tourist attraction and pretend it is your first time. Take notes and photos.
8. Eat leftovers by candlelight or dessert in your car by a river.
9. Surprise a child or forgive an enemy.
10. Give some of your money away anonymously or make a hat.

Chapter 33

Anger on a Dimmer Switch

Life can certainly be a four letter word if we do not know what to do with our emotions. Emotions, or feelings, can rise up within us like volcanic lava. Unlike a lava lamp, uncontained or mismanaged anger is not a pretty sight. When joy and happiness explode they come with confetti and streamers. When Anger goes BOOM it can come with pain and jail time.

Some handy dandy definitions

Spew: (Dr. Vali)
   To vomit
Tantrum: (Dr. Vali)
   To spew

Feelings are always okay. They are in themselves neutral and not subject to judgement. Feelings simply exist. Emotions are akin to the electrical force which comes through the wall outlets. Properly channelled, electrical force is a positive thing which provides resources for warmth and light and toasters. If, however, the channel has a short circuit, delay or interruption in flow, the snap, crackle, pop of flying sparks can create devastating fire. Burnt toast. The electricity itself is neutral, neither good nor bad.

Anger, like electricity, is a powerful force. Anger, directed in creative form has given the world great movements like the Reformation, Civil Rights, Democracy, and Education. Angry humans have created sociological events ranging from Holocaust to Civil Rights Marches. Indeed, it is the choices made with one's anger which end in creativity or carnage. Emotions are the colors that paint our realities and make us uniquely human. Feelings allow for discernment and clarity. It is not having feelings, but what we do with those feelings that can become a problem. The inappropriate or poorly planned manifestation of a particular feeling can lead to dangerous and even fatal consequences. Anger can be used for social and personal change. Anger can make great art. It brings us together or pulls us apart. The challenge of anger is not to deny, ignore or swallow up this powerful emotional force, but rather to find a way to express or manage it in a positive, creative and socially acceptable form.

We cannot CONTROL the emotional bubble ups of life annoyances, but we certainly have choices in how to manage them. If you get indigestion from an icky bite of food, the icky bubble has to either go up or down to get out...or it creates toxicity as it lies fetid and rotting inside. There is a grand difference between a polite burp and projectile vomiting. If you take the analogy to its farthest extremes, you can imagine what power can build up without appropriate relief measures. And watch out if you are in the way of someone's poorly managed eruption. Like I have told some of my clients in marital therapy, it is reasonable to release old pent up internal anger junk in the presence of a partner. It isn't reasonable to blow chunks on them. (Therapists learn how to hold the bucket and move back.)

It's a bit like learning to play the guitar. The novice spends time learning the basic techniques, then after practice and rehearsal, practice and rehearsal, more advanced skills are developed... There are countless Anger Management Experts available. Some are at mental health agencies, community colleges, hospitals or churches. There are many wonderful books on the market about anger management. Find one that suits you. A creative response brings us to our best and most fully alive state of being human. Create your own management list and post it on your refrigerator or car dash board. Seek fun, silly, non-violent, and safe ways to express feelings. (And remember, kids have bad days too, and can be guided into non-violent ways to squirt out their anger juices.) No one should have to swallow poison and keep quiet. But raging does not get the job done.

Survival tips de jour

1. Give yourself permission to feel your feelings and then consider your MANY choices.
2. Take a moment or two to ask yourself what you want and need.
3. Ask yourself "what am I a victim of, and do I have any power to change this situation?"

4. Ask yourself "what or who have I lost Faith in that pushed me into such Fear?"
5. Take a Walk until your anger goes bye-bye and you can figure out a positive plan.
6. Rip up old newspapers, but nothing else. Draw or color or paint pictures of your truth.
7. Announce that you are going to scream for a few moments and then go to a safe place which will not harm you or others and do so. Do not use words that hurt or blame...make animal sounds.
8. Do your laundry. And everyone else's. Put on warm socks, or a warm-just-out-of-the-dryer-blanket and wear a hat.
9. Sweep the house, driveway, garage, sidewalk, street, garage, porch...and even the yard if necessary.
10. Take a shower and let your feelings go down the drain.
11. Write your feelings on a brown paper bag, blow it up and then pop it.
12. Count to 10 and then 20 and then 63 Kazillion if needed.
13. Take a bath in the hottest water you can stand and let your feelings go down the drain.
14. Pound your mattress (not recommended for water beds).
15. Sing a very angry song using only words that describe your feelings and not using words that will hurt, blame or frighten anyone else.
16. Stomp through 14 mud puddles (if not available go kick leaves) (but don't kick anything else).

17. Wash the car, truck, driveway, or hose down the lawn or house or garage.
18. Do calisthenics, push-ups, jumping jacks, jog.
19. Do yoga, meditation, Tai-Chi or breathing exercises.
20. Sing, chant, cry, talk to yourself, affirm, pray, dance.
21. Take a break and sit on a porch swing. Pick flowers.
22. Write out all your feelings, then tear up the paper into itsy-bitsy-teensy-weensy pieces.
23. Call everyone in your support system and ask their permission to share your feelings. If they say no, respect that and find a teddy bear, cat, dog or horse who will listen to your feelings. But only expect the teddy bear to really listen carefully.
24. Release your anger energy back into the universe, thank it and bless it. Offer it back to the Source to be recycled as love and peace.
25. Work to resolve your issues by thinking, communicating and negotiating new choices.
26. Get professional help if necessary.

Chapter 34

Depression is so Depressing

Depression is a hole in the ground. It can be a hole that feels so deep and bottomless that the fall itself is beyond horror. But, once you land....it's just a hole.

Some handy dandy definitions

Bungee jumping: (Contemporary)
    A recreational activity which includes leaping off some edifice or structure while attached to an elastic cord
Bungee jumping: (Dr. Vali)
    Way nuts and a Chiropractor's dream come true

Okay. You're depressed. Now what? Life has provided you with the opportunity to fall into a hole. Wanna stay? Or climb out? Your choice. Some would rather sit on the bottom of the hole than go through the excruciating climb back up to light. When I hang out with someone who is depressed, I sit on the edge of the hole, holler down to them for a while and invite them back up to the Light. If they are interested I show them some of the twigs they can use to haul themselves out. I point out hand holds and a few rocks they can stand on to rest. I know that getting out is hard work. I wait to see if they want to go through the effort.

My philosophy: It isn't the hole that's the problem. The difficulty lies in memorizing your way back up. Because then, if you fall again, you aren't stuck there for 18-39 years. You can fall in the hole easily, or be pushed into one if you lose a job or loved one. The key is knowing that you don't need to move your furniture into the abyss.

I visualize the edge of the hole as a very dangerous and slippery area. It looks different to everyone. For example, the anniversary of my daughter Kirsha's death is slippery territory for me. So is Mother's Day. A friend found her slippery edge. She slipped each time she had to drive past her ex-husband's new house. The memories just elbowed her off the ledge and into the blackness of her abyss. You may start the slide when experiencing PMS or going for a job interview. Maybe it's on a holiday or when the kids grow up. It's when we are most vulnerable that we move toward the hole. Close to the hole the edges are not stable. The slip can be easy for the novice. Most days, the ground is level and safe. Then, suddenly, for no apparent reason, you start sliding downhill to the edge of the hole. Sometimes, it just appears easier to go with the emotional gravity and fall into it. It may seem that no matter what you do at this point a horrible fall over the cliff is inevitable.

It isn't.

Some folks just give up and yell wheeeeeeeeeeeeeeeeeeee as they career over the edge into the chasm. Some reach for straws to hang onto. I suggest a depression bungee cord.

About 200 yards from the edge of every hole is a very strong and ancient tree. It is the anchor of your faith and belief. Tie a cord of hope and memory to that tree, wrap it around your heart and bounce back up. It is useful to have your own cord well secured before you try to help anyone else who has fallen into their abyss. If you have ever tried to rescue people, you know that they can pull you into their hole then climb over you to get back to the light. ICK. Then **you** are down in the hole.

What is your cord? For some it is God. For others it is the smiles of their children. For some it is the knowledge that life is temporary, and for others it is the love of a spouse or family system. Others find their source of light in nature or literature, while others find it in their own will to live. **The tree** which your cord is tied to is that unshakable place which establishes your own powerful faith. The place where fear cannot reside. Absolutely. **The cord** is the link between that faith and your day to day walk on Planet Earth. **The tug** is your reach back to the belief that everything is fine, even in the face of the bellowing open mouth of the seductive hole.

True healing from simple depression seems manifest when one not only tugs on the cord and gets back to the tree, but can move beyond that tree into an even more distant perspective of the hole and serve others. The hole loses its power when you can come and go as you please. The darkness becomes just a memory shadow. The light has become more appealing. The trip back to light has become more familiar.

If you do slip over the cliff you may simply land on the first ledge. Don't leap all the way to the bottom just because you fell over the edge....tug the cord. If you slip over the cliff and bounce off the first ledge onto a deeper ledge...pull the cord. If you land at the bottom, hopeless and lost...find your map, take a deep breath, and climb out. Even if you have misplaced your cord of hope and faith, crawl up the steep cliff back to the light.

If you enjoy, crave, or are addicted to mud, dank, darkness, and grubby crawly things that live in the muck, I wish you well. Take your furniture. But if you like laughter and celebration and flowers and butterflies and sugar cookies......come to the top and play. Come as you are. Even if you are still covered with mud, remember that the light and warmth dries up the goo and it will eventually blow off like ancient dust.

Survival tips de jour

1. Keep a list of all the good things that happen to you in a special Bliss Book to refer to during days of darkness.
2. Make a list of resources of friends and loved ones who aren't in the hole...ask them how they stay out.
3. Remember that feeling blue doesn't mean you are at the bottom.
4. Everything is Temporary.
5. Take a $20 bill. Staple a note to it that reads: "This money proves I am never broke" Don't spend it. Ever.
6. List 10 things that make your heart soar.
7. Bless and forgive 10 things that make your heart sore.
8. One great cure for depression is to do something kind for someone else... anonymously.
9. Depression can be anger turned inside out....find out what you may be angry about.
10. Choose Faith and not Fear... always.

Note: Depression can signify a serious medical or mental health condition which needs evaluation and treatment from a qualified medical professional. If you have questions about depression, refer them to your physician or a qualified mental health professional.

Chapter 35

So Sorry

I'm sorry, I forgot to mention how apologizing can be a survival skill. Just like learning a musical instrument, it takes a lot of practice and rehearsal to create harmony. I should make amends for not mentioning this sooner. I hope you will forgive me quickly and take me off the hook for being so human again. Sometimes it is just annoying to be human.

Some Handy Dandy Definitions

Amend: (Webster)
    To put right
Amend: (Dr. Vali)
    Change
Change: (Dr. Vali)
    Transform

I was having coffee and the barista asked me how I was and I offered the traditional, "fine," which was countered with "and you?" which was responded to with "oh, I have a cold," to which I graciously responded, "oh, I'm sorry," to which he weirdly responded, "oh, it's not your fault." I took my coffee to my table and thought about it. Was it my fault that he had a cold? Somehow the words, "I'm sorry" suggested to him some sort of accountability for his virus. Now I was very clear that his virus had nothing to do with me, but rather the fact that he was a human being who was vulnerable. And indeed it is very risky to be human on a day to day basis. I then began tedious contemplations of how apologizing is the essence of survival. Apologizing acknowledges to ourselves and others that we are human. Being human means we are always at risk. It occurred to me that people who can't apologize must be under the illusion that they are either above or beyond human frailty. Perhaps they are shaking a magic ju-ju over their own heads hoping they can escape the inevitable accountability of making their own soul choices. They must be truly living in fear. How scary for them.

Making amends, apologizing and offering up our vulnerability is not about our relationship with other people as much as it is about our relationship with whoever runs the universe, which I happen to think is God. When we get to the next world, whatever our belief is about that, the gatekeepers will probably only ask one question, "Were you kind?" And since kindness has to do with humility, vulnerability, and service to other souls, there will probably be a little journal with hash marks for all the times we were brave enough to say, "Oops, that one was mine," or "Sorry about that, were those your little toes that got stepped on?" or "My apologies for being a grump." It's Scrooge taking the goose to the Cratchits but eating crow himself. In that

146

process he set himself free from invisible chains which he was creating himself.

In the emancipation boogie with my daughter, we sometimes find it difficult to offer up our vulnerability. Our apologizing rituals have taken some practice and now we are both good at it. We began by quoting a line from a movie we both saw where the arrogant but good hearted character struggled with an apology to someone. He was very awkward at it and could not quite be direct. We quoted his lines. That way we said, "Sorry," without having to take all the fear on our shoulders. Then the other could repeat the next line of the movie as an acknowledgment of its effect and we moved on. I don't know where people get the idea that saying the "s" word creates some sort of imbalance of power in a universe where we are all equal. Perhaps it increases the possibility that the poles will shift, global warming will increase and the price of cheese will collapse in world markets. Saying "I'm sorry" allows the recipient of those words to be generous and loving, graceful, compassionate and kind. Why would someone deny a friend the opportunity to bless them and increase their forgiveness skills? I think that people who don't apologize are thieves. They steal our humanity and our opportunity to forgive and forget. They pretend that they have some special place in the universe that keeps them protected from the terrors of our sacred truth – that we are temporary. But then again, I suppose I think too much. I'm sorry.

Survival Tips De Jour

1. Don't fear these letters of the alphabet: s-o-r-r-y.
2. Offer up your apology and allow others to offer up grace.
3. Make amends.
4. Don't apologize if it increases your own personal sense of martyrdom. No one needs that kind of apology.
5. Celebrate your vulnerability, it's all you've got.
6. Don't apologize for being yourself.
7. Don't apologize to dangerous people who use it to increase their distorted perception of power.
8. Do random acts of apology.
9. Be kind to yourself and apologize to your own heart while learning to laugh at your own humanness.
10. The only thing that matters is kindness.

Chapter 36

Another Chance

If success means getting up one more time than you fall on your face, then many human beings on the planet can call themselves a grand success. Every day we wake up we get another chance to change our hearts and our worlds. Other chances are a true key to survival.

Some Handy Dandy Definitions

Chance: (Webster)
    Something that happens unpredictably without discernible human intention or observable cause
Chance: (Dr. Vali)
    Opportunity given which may not be deserved but should be appreciated

If you have traveled with me via this column over the years, you know we have trekked through a soul journey. Sometimes our transportation has been by means of mystical rings. The **Magic Princess Ring** began our sojourn. We looked deep into it's illusion and followed our fantasies. When reality hit the fan we found the **Magic Toe Ring** and sat on a Maui Beach together to regroup from losses. We wiggled our feet in the glorious sand of soul discovery and came out into the sunlight just in time to be given the **Diamond of Truth Ring**. This ring promised more than a Princess Journey....it promised the Queenship. The journey has moved us onward and now there is a new ring to consider, the **Ring of Another Chance**. After yet another soul survivor close call I, your humble tour guide, was recently given this ring. I had been sitting having a cup of tea with Death again. When Death left suddenly for another assignment there was a new ring on my finger. It was a gift of love from my heart-hero. The power of this ring has the potential to transform both the bearer and the recipient from soul survivors to soul servants. The journey from Survivor to Servant moves the traveler from the Save-Myself-Mission which is initially necessary to stay alive to a place where one can begin rebuilding and serving others with survival tips. Once past the survival stage the seeker must turn around and care for others for the survival to matter. Just like the other rings, The **Ring of Another Chance** is jubilantly offered to you. Look into its glittery sparkle to find ways to transform your darkness, loss, pain and fear into brilliant, shining, light filled opportunities for service. There are huge winds of life which leave rubble in the streets. Who will clean it up? The survivors. The soul sweepers. It is now up to survivors to press on with the mission of humanity, the mission of charity, the mission of compassion.

There are events which change our lives and change our world. These events give us choices to think life is unfair, to wallow in our pain, to ignore their significance, to make jokes, to blame, to shame, to run and hide, to exploit, to tantrum, to whine, or remain a victim forever. Another choice is to stand in the presence of the Darkness and bless the Universe for giving us **Another Chance** to make a new and better choice or to be present for those who are just starting out in the battle to survive life. We can collectively keep vigil for the miracle which is sure to follow any devastation. After the pain and the longing, the terror and the anger, the grief and the sorrow, the vulnerability and the anguish, there is a place where there you will find two doors. One is marked victim and the other is marked light. The light door is for Soul Survivors.

I invite you to place the **Ring of Another Chance** upon your finger, toe, earlobe, nose, hairwrap, or lapel and take **Another Chance** to make a difference. Let's keep moving along on the tour my dear fellow travelers, but pay close attention now, I think the next part of the journey is going to be amazing.

Survival Tips De Jour

1. Give yourself Another Chance.
2. Don't take chances.
3. Take a chance.
4. If Death is in your living room, make tea, it might leave.
5. If someone has given you another chance, honor it as grace.
6. Service to others is no service if you feel like a righteous victim or martyr. Nobody needs that kind of help.
7. Give service anonymously sometimes.
8. Thank service providers when they provide you service.
9. If you lost at love give yourself another chance.
10. Bless all Sweepers.

Final Thoughts

Survival is a tricky business. It includes physical, emotional, and spiritual elements. I have seen films and read texts about cultures who have had great droughts or catastrophes, suffered horrendous social catastrophes, and have either survived as a culture or disappeared. Some disappear because of the loss of art and ritualism, others because of the loss of spirit.

I recall vivid images of indigenous people sitting beside their huts with sticks in their hands. They would push the dirt about from side to side with the stick. They had lost so much that day after day all they could manage was to move bits of dirt back and forth. They had lost spirit and creativity, and I suspect a sense of humor. They were so used up that they could offer nothing more to their culture. Eventually there was nothing more. This led me to believe that there is "survival" and then there is SURVIVAL .

If there is no soul, no spirit, no humor...then there is no point. My life challenges have been

153

profound, and yet, I'm not headed for that little stick to push the dirt. I hope I have offered another option to those who are also challenged.

These humble writings come from my soul's striving. I offer them to you. Thank you for reading.

Vali Hawkins Mitchell, PhD

About the Author

Vali Hawkins Mitchell, PhD, co-owner of Inner Directions Counseling and Education Services in Richland, Washington, is an author, consultant, Certified Mental Health Counselor, performance artist, writing teacher, researcher, educational trainer and freelance writer. She has done primary medical research which has received international attention and is a well published writer in both professional and art press. Dr. Hawkins Mitchell has advanced training in Critical Incident Stress Debriefing and Disaster Management and provides services to individuals and businesses which have survived any form of trauma or want pre-incident training.

She travels extensively providing seminars on a variety of issues in the field of Health Education. Seminar titles have included topics on Pre-Disaster Crisis Training for Managers, Mental Health First Aid for Professionals, Living Well with Chronic Illness, Parenting Children with Chronic Illness, Diabetes Management for Kids and Parents, Music and Emotions, Dreamworking, Anger Management, Creativity and Survival, Parenting After Divorce, Teambuilding and Critical Incident Stress Management for Health Professionals, Creative Writing in Business, and an original series on Free Writing.

She is a regular contributing writer to Simon and Schuster, a playwright, and has written a number of award winning scores for Children's Theater, and a column for INKFISH Magazine.

155

Dr. Vali is available for speaking engagements, conferences, and workshops throughout the country and offers a wide range of topics. Her presentations are enlightening, educational, entertaining and upbeat. She brings her audiences, students and workshop participants to a new level of awareness and takes them on a journey of self discovery with her stories and ideas.

Vali Hawkins Mitchell, Ph.D., C.M.H.C.
Inner Directions Counseling and Education Services
2815 W. Van Giesen
Richland, WA 99352
509-942-0443
vali@owt.com